TLC

TEACHING & LEADING CHILDREN

Training for Supportive Guidance of Children Under Six

A STEP *handbook for early childhood teachers*

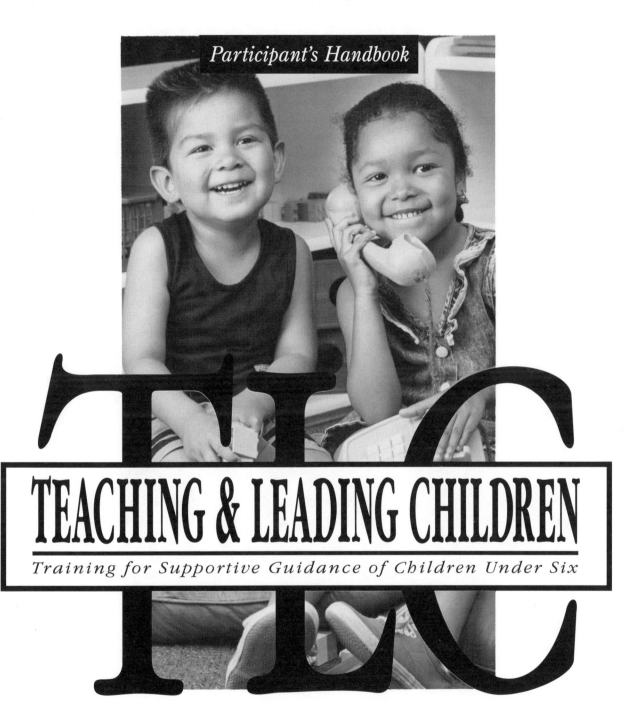

Participant's Handbook

TEACHING & LEADING CHILDREN

Training for Supportive Guidance of Children Under Six

Don Dinkmeyer, Ph.D.   Gary D. McKay, Ph.D.   James S. Dinkmeyer, M.A.   Don Dinkmeyer, Jr., Ph.D.

American Guidance Service, Inc., Circle Pines, Minnesota 55014-1796

AGS staff participating in the development
and production of this publication:

Project Team   Marjorie Lisovskis and Teri Mathews, Senior Editors

Christopher Weber, Designer

Theodore Remington, Assistant Editor

Project Editor   Joan Brooks

Cartoons   John Bush

Cover Photo   Scott Jacobson

Photographs   Mark Langenfeld: p. 10. Michael Sulik: pp. 10, 135, 152. Martha Tabor: pp. 11, 75. Cleo Photography: p. 47. Tom Brownold: p. 51. Jim West: pp. 85, 104. Bett Adams: p. 121. Steve Niedorf: pp. 136, 188.

> To early childhood teachers and caregivers
> who are shaping the future every day

© 1992 **AGS**® American Guidance Service, Inc.

Printed in the United States of America

A 0 9 8 7 6 5

Library of Congress Catalog Card Number 07-72787

ISBN 0-88671-464-8

Contents

Acknowledgments

Many people contributed to the development and production of *Teaching and Leading Children*. We wish to acknowledge with appreciation:

E. Jane Dinkmeyer, Dr. Joyce L. McKay, Lyn Dinkmeyer, and Deb Dinkmeyer, who provided technical assistance and professional insight as well as love, support, and encouragement.

The many early childhood teachers, staff, and consultants who provided valuable feedback in the early stages of development, including Kay Martin, Terry Webb, Kate Whitaker, and Yolanda Uribe, all from Tucson, Arizona; Kathy Walton of Columbia, South Carolina; Judith D. Snyder of Cary, Illinois; Charlene C. Wenc of Burr Ridge, Illinois; and Jan Hardy and her staff, Coral Springs, Florida.

Mary Bregman, Coral Springs, Florida and Mary Carlyon, Tucson, Arizona, who typed, retyped, photocopied, and mailed through many drafts of the manuscript.

Diane McLinn, Minneapolis, Minnesota, who contributed dozens of examples based on the experience of herself and her co-teachers.

The many field testers who provided honest and helpful feedback regarding their experiences with the field-test edition of the book. Special thanks to Patricia Griffin, Camden, New Jersey, for contributing an example for Chapter 6.

Dr. Verna Hildebrand, Professor in the Department of Family and Child Ecology at Michigan State University, East Lansing, Michigan, who provided a thoughtful and thorough critique of the field-test manuscript.

Arnetta Whitfield, Director of Educational Services for the Child Care Connection of Broward County, Fort Lauderdale, Florida, whose staff critiqued the field-test manuscript.

Joan Brooks, St. Paul, Minnesota, who worked with diligence and sensitivity to bring the work of many into a single clear voice.

John Bush, Minneapolis, Minnesota, who created the clever cartoon illustrations.

Especially, we thank the late Rudolf Dreikurs, from whom we learned much of what we know about teachers, parents, and children.

Don Dinkmeyer
Gary D. McKay
James S. Dinkmeyer
Don Dinkmeyer, Jr.
September, 1992

Introduction

Welcome to TLC

As a teacher of young children, you are a major influence in their lives. Your teaching helps children build a healthy foundation for their approach to life and learning. You do this in two ways—by the knowledge you help children gain about the world, and by the ways in which you relate to each child.

The principles and skills you will learn in *TLC—Teaching and Leading Children*—can help you feel more confident in your work. The book suggests a positive and consistent approach. It is based on the widely used parenting programs called *STEP—Systematic Training for Effective Parenting,* and *Early Childhood STEP. TLC* applies *STEP*'s principles and methods to the special challenges of working with infants, toddlers, and preschoolers in an educational or child care setting. This book can be your partner as you work to build healthy patterns of belief, behavior, and learning in young children.

TLC provides the following skills to increase your effectiveness as a teacher.

- **Understanding children's individual rates and styles of development**. Effective early childhood specialists understand how young children grow and develop. Children don't necessarily match developmental charts as they grow—each child develops at his or her own rate. Being aware of the individuality of each child is important. To teach children well, you need to know what can reasonably be expected from

1

each child and how best to help children grow in each developmental stage.

- **Understanding the difference between troublesome behavior that is normal and true misbehavior.** There is an important difference between troublesome behavior that occurs in children as a result of developmental factors—such as the need to assert independence—and misbehavior, which arises out of a child's attempt to belong when positive actions don't get results. In *TLC* you will learn the four goals of children's misbehavior. Understanding the purpose of a child's troublesome behavior is the first step in responding effectively and positively.

- **Listening for children's feelings and real meanings, and communicating your own feelings respectfully.** We all talk with children, but there are ways to speak and listen to them that are especially helpful. Tuning in to children's feelings helps them feel understood and valued. When we respectfully communicate our feelings to children about how their behavior affects us, children learn effective ways of sharing their feelings with others. By modeling effective communication, teachers help children learn communication skills that are important for their personal and social development.

- **Using the process of encouragement to build self-esteem.** All children need encouragement. Encouragement builds their self-esteem. When you accept children as they are, communicate your faith in them, and build on their strengths, you are teaching them they are lovable and capable. You help them become prepared to meet life's challenges.

- **Recognizing problem ownership.** We adults often tend to assume responsibility for all the problems children have. But even young children can learn to "own" and take care of some of the problems they create or encounter in their lives. While we as teachers are always there to guide and assist children, helping them learn to own their problems helps them develop self-confidence and responsibility.

- **Helping children solve problems.** Through a process called exploring alternatives, you will learn how to help children develop their problem-solving abilities. The process is an effective group guidance approach that can be used for problem solving between you and children, and for handling conflicts among children.

- **Applying appropriate discipline methods.** Discipline is a major challenge for teachers of young children. Effective discipline is guidance—an educational process—not a tool to force obedience. The desired goal of discipline is to promote self-discipline and responsibility in children, which enable them to cooperate with others.

2

- **Understanding and guiding children's emotional and social development.** You will learn to apply *TLC* methods to emotional and social challenges, such as temper tantrums and separation anxiety, that often arise as children develop.

- **Working with parents.** You and the parents are partners in teaching and leading children. Most parents have a strong investment in their children—they want the best for them. But parents may have different ideas about methods or goals. If you have a sound, developmentally appropriate program, and clearly communicate your goals and the reasons for your methods to parents, most will accept your efforts. *TLC* gives suggestions for enlisting parents' cooperation and participation.

In addition to helping you with children and parents, *TLC* gives you opportunities to increase your own interpersonal skills and self-esteem. The "Just For You" activities focus on you as a person, with your own beliefs, feelings, and relationships that extend into your life beyond your role as a teacher.

Working with young children is always a challenge. It is also full of opportunities. Both teachers and children experience many joys and satisfactions as the children grow. Whether you are studying *TLC* in a group or on your own, it can help you meet the challenge—and the opportunities—with confidence.

Chapter 1
Understanding Children's Development and Behavior

What You Will Learn

- Children develop at their own rates and in their own styles.

- Not all troublesome behavior is misbehavior.

- Children's misbehavior has one of four goals: attention, power, revenge, or display of inadequacy.

- You can encourage positive behavior goals by doing the unexpected and by focusing on the positive.

Giving Children a Good Start in Life

While parents and other family members are children's first teachers, early childhood educators are important partners in a child's development. As a person who works in the field of early childhood education, your job is a very important one. You may actually spend more hours each day with some of the children than their family adults are able to do at home. You are dealing with many children at once, all with their own individual needs and personalities.

Your job as an early childhood teacher* will bring you challenge, stress, and great reward. There will be many opportunities to

*In *Teaching and Leading Children* we use the titles *teacher* or *early childhood staff* to refer to all who work with babies, toddlers, or preschoolers in early childhood settings, including preschools, early childhood centers, and family day care homes. Many of the concepts are relevant to teachers of kindergarten children as well.

influence the development of the children in your care. You will want to work as a partner with parents and others to provide the best start in life for them.

Young children need caring, nurturing teachers and early childhood staff who understand children's behavior and provide an environment suited to their special needs and levels of development. *Teaching and Leading Children* will help you learn what practices are appropriate for the children you teach.

In this chapter, we'll look at children's behavior in two ways—in terms of developmental expectations, and in terms of purpose.

- **Developmental expectations** are behaviors and accomplishments teachers can generally expect from children at certain ages.

- **Purpose** refers to children's natural desires to explore and learn about their world, and the reasons for their misbehavior when they become discouraged.

Each Child's Development Is Individual and Unique

Each child has a particular temperament—a behavioral style—and an individual rate of development. These built-in traits reveal themselves as children grow. Effective teachers work *with* these individual qualities rather than trying to change them.

Temperament

Each child is born with an individual temperament that stays basically the same throughout childhood.[1] Temperament has nothing to do with intelligence or talent. It refers to the unique qualities a child is born with.

Temperament is the unique set of qualities and characteristics an individual child is born with.

> *It's early morning and parents are dropping children off in the toddler room. Eighteen-month-old LaTanya squeals in delight and waddles away from her father to join her classmates. Twenty-month-old Brandon clings to his mother's legs and peers warily at the other children. Brandon's teacher greets him quietly and helps ease the transition from home to center by holding him in her lap until he's ready to play.*

Some children are active, others are quiet. Some infants get hungry and sleepy at regular times, others are unpredictable. Some easily accept loud noises, bright lights, and new tastes. Others are upset by changes in their environment.

> *In the infant room, the teacher is introducing two children to the taste of mashed bananas. Clem opens his mouth wide to accept the spoonful of bananas and smacks his lips afterwards. Annie turns her face aside when the spoon approaches. After accepting a tiny bite, Annie oozes the bananas out of her mouth.*

Each child's style is a reflection of individual temperament. When we recognize and accept each child's temperament as a given, we gain a deeper understanding of the child. This can help us appreciate and work with each child's particular style.

Rate of Development

Children develop at their own rates. Each has an individual timetable for reaching the milestones of development. Cutting teeth is an event largely preset in each child at birth. To a certain extent, the time for starting to crawl, learning to talk, and being ready for toilet training are preset, too. But these tasks are also influenced by a child's experience in the world. For example, adult attempts to speed up a child's development can discourage the child and actually slow the process down.

> *Four-year-old Elizabeth is learning how to write her name. At school, her teacher encourages her to try writing any of the letters in her name that she knows. At home, her older brother teases her for printing the letters backwards and out of order. Soon Elizabeth stops practicing her name at school and asks the teacher to write it for her because "it's too hard."*

Style of Development

Children develop in their own styles, too. Some children are enthusiastic about learning. They will try out skills in front of the other children and not worry about making mistakes. Other children are more cautious, wanting to make sure they have mastered something before trying it in public. Some infants and toddlers happily babble nonsense syllables for months before they say anything that sounds like real words. Others wait until they can say a whole sentence before they speak much at all. Some children seem to develop physically, emotionally, intellectually, and socially all at the same time. Others appear to develop skills in one area at a time.

Effective teachers work <u>with</u> children's individual qualities, rather than trying to change them.

7

Five-year-old Jason can swing hand-over-hand across the monkey bars and does cartwheels easily. On the playground, he often leads his classmates in superhero play where he can show off his physical skills. However, in the preschoolers' room Jason is struggling to learn how to identify shapes.

Teachers help children by respecting their rates of development. It is our job to see, appreciate, and offer chances for children to develop, but not to push them.

Stages of Development

Development is sequential—it occurs in a certain order. Certain skills must be present before others can be developed. For example, large and small motor skills must be developed before a child can learn to read and write, because reading and writing require eye-hand coordination.

Children develop gradually, rather than in abrupt steps. You may have seen developmental charts (such as Chart 1A at the end of this chapter) showing average ages at which a child will do various tasks. This kind of information is important. It helps us understand a lot about children's abilities and behavior as they grow. But it is critical to recognize that, as individuals, children are never "average." At any age, a child may differ from the charts in some or all categories. However, if a child is considerably behind agemates, it might be time to bring this to the attention of a parent or guardian and suggest professional help.

Three-year-old Kristin has been in an early childhood center for over a year. Her words seem limited to "no" and "mine." Kristin has a history of frequent ear infections. After observing Kristin's lack of speech progress, her teacher meets with Kristin's father. She suggests he consult with the family doctor about any potential hearing loss that might be affecting Kristin's speech development.

Teachers help children by respecting their rates of development. It is our job to see, appreciate, and offer chances for children to develop, but *not to push them*. This means providing a safe, developmentally appropriate environment for children, and opportunities for them to explore and learn. We avoid trying to push them into developing skills before they are ready. (For example, expecting a two-year-old to tie shoes, or a five-year-old to understand multiplication.)

Babies are explorers.

Developmental Periods

Teaching and Leading Children covers three developmental periods: infancy, toddlerhood, and preschool.

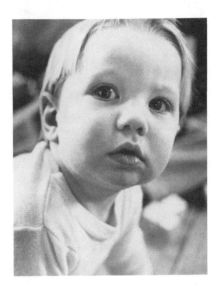

Infants—Newborns to Eighteen Months*

Infants are learning to trust other human beings. They learn to count on others to care for them and provide protection, limits, and fun. They are learning that someone will:

- take care of their basic physical needs.
- listen and respond to their wails of protest.
- stop them from moving toward danger.

Infants are also learning to trust themselves to take care of some of their own needs. They are learning to recognize that they can:

- comfort themselves with a thumb or a special blanket.
- get what they want by crawling and grasping.
- enjoy themselves by finding their toes or fists to chew on.

Infants are learning to trust their environments. We want to help them discover that the world is sometimes predictable and sometimes surprising, but basically safe.

- The floor is hard, stuffed animals are soft.
- Orange food tastes good, green food is questionable.
- Water feels good, but a wet diaper doesn't.

*Each age range is meant to be a general guideline. For example, for some children infancy ends at fifteen months; then they enter toddlerhood.

Toddlers—Eighteen Months to Three Years

Toddlers are reaching for independence. Once children have learned to trust, they are ready to test their independence. Toddlers search for independence in a variety of ways. Each act of independence teaches them about various human traits.

- They insist on doing everything for themselves (and are learning the trait of self-reliance).
- They are likely to lay claim to all objects in the area (ownership).
- They may fear the unfamiliar (insecurity).
- They can handle pets gently (self-control).

In these and many other ways, toddlers are taking major steps toward growing up.

Preschoolers—Three to Five Years

Preschoolers are beginning to show creativity.
Preschoolers have formed both trust and independence in their basic relationships. Now they enter an expanding world of friends and toys. Preschoolers are artists, inventors, and manufacturers. An environment that includes dolls, building toys, balls, sand, water, paint, picture books, and other familiar materials encourages their budding imaginations and a desire to learn about the world.

Preschoolers start to use language for complicated stories. They create stories of their own and delight in listening to you tell or read them as well. Words themselves become fascinating. Children invent their own silly ones and rhyme for the fun of rhyming. They may feel the excitement of shocking an unsuspecting teacher with a swear word.

Preschoolers need friends. They are ready to learn how people get along. With friends, preschoolers practice using ideas, making decisions, settling arguments, showing appreciation, and practicing adult roles by playing house, school, or doctor.

Some four and five-year-olds may already be in kindergarten. But that doesn't change the fact that they are still young children. At this age, they still likely think and behave more like younger children who are not yet in school.[2]

Your Role in Influencing Children

The way we relate to children influences their most basic feelings about themselves and others.

Teaching Styles

There are three general styles in which adults often relate to children—*autocratic, permissive, and democratic*. Each style has different consequences for the children's development.

Autocratic style—limits without freedom. Adults who follow an autocratic style depend on rewards and punishments to control children. An autocratic teacher might say, "You can't go out to the playground today because you didn't help clean up the room." Punishment stimulates fear and resentment in children. And if you rely heavily on rewards, children may come to expect payment for cooperative behavior.

An autocratic atmosphere may produce a rigid, too-quiet playroom or learning center environment. This kind of atmosphere can lead to unhappiness and stress in children, even though it may look outwardly calm and orderly to adults who like things that way.

Permissive style—freedom without limits. Teachers who use a permissive style set few or no limits on behavior. They offer children a lot of freedom, but give them no responsibility. A permissive teacher might ask the children to help clean up the room, but then do it herself if they don't cooperate. This kind of atmosphere gives children an unrealistic view of how the world works. Children with no limits on their behavior often exhibit out-of-control, aggressive behavior.

Democratic style—freedom within limits. Democratic teaching is based on equality and mutual respect. It encourages responsibility. A teacher who follows a democratic style might be heard to say, "We can go out to play after we pick up the toys."

Equality does not mean sameness. No two people are the same, but they are equal in terms of human worth and dignity. The democratic method doesn't mean giving young children the same freedom and responsibilities as older children or adults. It *does* mean giving their desires equal consideration. It doesn't mean children make all the decisions. It *does* mean encouraging them to help make decisions within limits. For example:

- Children can be encouraged to choose materials for art projects or writing activities.

- Although they are not allowed to choose the time when lunch is served, children may be encouraged to choose whether to have apple or banana as part of their meal.

Development is sequential—it occurs in a certain order. Certain skills must be present before others can be developed.

From infancy through the early childhood years, children need secure boundaries. Their ability to make choices develops gradually over time. Very young children can't depend on themselves to keep the rules. They need you to set boundaries. For example, a group of toddlers can't be expected to share a plate of crackers evenly at snack time. They need an adult to divide the crackers so each child gets an equal share.

Teaching and Leading Children is based on democratic principles. These principles allow young children *choices within limits* and also help them to learn personal responsibility. It is the most effective system for preparing children to live in a democracy where responsibility will be expected of them. As you study each part of *Teaching and Leading Children,* you will learn how to use democratic principles in dealing with the children in your care.

The Power of Expectations

As teachers, we all have certain expectations of the children we work with. Unfortunately, it is all too easy to expect negative behavior from them. You've probably heard such terms as "terrible twos," "rug rats," and "little monsters." Even if adults use these labels jokingly, they lead us to expect problems with children. *Expectations are powerful.* Young children sense our expectations. They often believe them and act accordingly.

For example, many toddler teachers encounter problems with children who bite. If a teacher clearly lets children know that she expects them to handle conflicts with words instead of aggressive actions, she will probably have fewer biting incidents to deal with than a teacher whose only strategy is to isolate the biter on a time-out chair after the fact. (For a more complete discussion of biting, see Chapter 5.)

Because two-year-olds are asserting independence, it's easy to interpret everything they do as an effort to gain power or control. But relationships with toddlers don't always have to turn into power struggles. Consider how relationships with two-year-olds would be different if we only heard about the "terrific twos"! The more positive your expectations of children, the more likely it is that you will get cooperation from them. When we are positive, we help build an important foundation of self-esteem that will affect children's emotional development for life.

Providing More "Yes" than "No" Experiences

"No" is the young toddler's favorite word. Toddlers may say no when they actually mean yes. One reason toddlers say no so much may be because they hear it over and over from the adults in their lives.

We suggest you work to say no less often. One way to do this is to provide choices for children as an alternative to using the word no. A choice may rule out one kind of behavior, but it offers others as substitutes. For example, two children might want to play chase indoors. You may have to stop them for safety reasons. But you can say yes to the behavior by giving them the choice to go outside. Or you can suggest a different indoor activity instead.

Certainly, there are times when saying no is necessary. For example, if a toddler pulls her* hand away and runs ahead while crossing the street, a teacher might say:

- "No—we always hold hands and we don't run in the street. We want everyone to be safe."

Motor skills are physical abilities requiring a certain amount of strength, coordination, or dexterity.
Large motor skills involve larger muscle groups, small motor skills involve smaller muscle groups.

---

* In *Teaching and Leading Children*, the use of masculine and feminine pronouns is varied throughout. The information presented, however, applies to children of either sex.

13

Or a child may ask whether he can do something and you may have to say no. But you could let the child experience a yes by redirecting him to another activity. There are often opportunities to literally say yes instead of no. For example, "No, you mustn't hug so hard!" could be stated,

- "Yes, I like hugs too. But you need to hug John gently."

The point is to keep no to a minimum and to use yes as much as possible. This is true even in cases where the immediacy of the moment may seem to prompt a quick "NO!"—if, for instance, a toddler picks up a toy and tries to hit another child with it. A better response is to remove the toy, saying:

- "Christina, we don't hit people. Hitting hurts."

Then help the child deal with the problem that led to the aggressive feelings in the first place.

Why Children Behave As They Do

The following principles of human behavior can help us understand children—and ourselves.

Humans are social beings. Very early on, we discover life involves living with other people.

The main goal in life is to belong. As human beings, we need to find our place among other people. Early childhood is a time for discovering how to belong. As young children grow and develop, they discover certain responses from others give a feeling of belonging. They also learn they get different kinds of responses through cooperative and uncooperative behavior.

Children develop at their own individual rates and in their own styles. Each child will master new skills when she or he is ready.

> *Two-year-old Hai intently watches his teacher wiping the table after lunch. "Me help?" he asks. His teacher smiles and says, "Yes, Hai. I'd like it if you'd help me," and hands him the sponge. Hai happily wipes off the table and proceeds to wash the chairs, too. His teacher tells him how much she appreciates his help and Hai claps for himself.*

Behavior is goal directed—it is done for a purpose. Observing the activity of young children reveals that their behavior has a purpose. Watch an infant explore a new object placed in his crib. He fondles it and tastes it—trying to discover the nature of the object. Watch an older child build a tower. Her purpose may be to represent a part of the world she is familiar with—such as a tall building. The child may also be testing her skills.

Behavior serves a purpose, whether it's positive or negative. For example, if a three-year-old becomes defiant when you ask for cooperation, he has a goal—to demonstrate his power by means of that defiance.

Behavior and Misbehavior

It's very important to keep in mind that not all behavior we find troublesome can be classified as misbehavior. With very young children, there are generally two kinds of "problem" behavior.

1. **Developmentally appropriate behavior we may find troublesome.** Certain bothersome behaviors can be expected from most children at certain ages and stages of development. For example, infants cry to be fed. We may find the crying bothersome, but we can't classify it as misbehavior. In fact, the crying is the infant's only way of letting adults know she is hungry. When a two-year-old tracks mud across the floor, it may be because he doesn't know that muddy shoes leave a dirty trail. Or he may be fascinated by what he's able to do with his shoes, without any negative or careless intent.

Sometimes children "misbehave" simply because they are curious, tired, sick, clumsy, trying to be helpful, or don't know the rules. In these cases, the behavior we find troublesome isn't misbehavior at all. We may simply have unrealistic expectations.

The democratic method doesn't mean giving young children the same responsibilities as older children or adults. It does mean giving their desires equal consideration.

> *The teacher in the four-year-old room is reading and teaching about spiders at circle time. Although spiders are interesting to preschoolers, the group has been sitting and listening for twenty minutes. Carlos gets bored and starts pinching Lydia. She lets out a howl and the whole group turns its attention towards her. The teacher realizes the children have been sitting a long time and says, "Let's all stand up and move around like giant spiders."*

2. **Misbehavior.** Misbehavior can be defined as *the failure to cooperate when the child knows how to cooperate and is able to do so.* For example, a four-year-old crying and fussing during snack time may behave that way to gain attention or protest what's being served. This can be uncooperative behavior if the child knows better and his behavior is disturbing others. On the other hand, if the child is sick or frightened, such behavior might be understood differently.

Another example of uncooperative misbehavior is the five-year-old who drops her coat and backpack on the floor the minute she enters the kindergarten room, even though her teacher has repeatedly shown her how to hang them up on a hook.

Any behavior which knowingly endangers a child's own safety, or that of others, is another form of misbehavior. The word "knowingly" is important here. Children learn about danger over time. Toddlers may not understand the potential consequences of dangerous behavior the same way preschoolers do.

Why Children Misbehave

Children generally misbehave for two reasons—because they are discouraged, and because their negative behavior is reinforced by those around them.

Discouragement. Most children want to cooperate. But if they feel they can't achieve belonging through cooperative behavior, they may become discouraged and misbehave in order to find a way they *can* belong. If, for example, a child does not achieve attention through doing something positive, she may then discover she can gain attention through behavior that gets a negative response.

The late Rudolf Dreikurs, noted psychiatrist, lecturer, and author, said something very important when he commented: "A misbehaving child is a discouraged child."

Reinforcement. Children can "misbehave" without intending to. How we respond to one or two incidents can influence what behaviors children repeat and how often they repeat them. Through our responses, we give children ideas on how to belong.

Two-and-a-half-year-old Eric accidentally knocks over his juice cup at snack time. The teacher, who is busy with another child at that moment, reacts with a flurry of paper towels. She then pours more juice into Eric's cup and moves back to the child she was talking to. A few moments later, Eric's juice is spilled again. This time, it is not an accident.

In this situation, Eric is experimenting with being uncooperative as a way of gaining attention and a feeling of belonging. Realizing this, Eric's teacher takes a different approach to the second spill. She treats it as an opportunity for Eric to learn responsibility.

Looking over at an aide, the teacher calmly says, "Arlene, would you please get Eric a sponge," and goes on with what she is doing. The aide hands Eric a sponge and asks him to help clean up the table.

Young children sense our expectations. They often believe them and act accordingly.

In this way, Eric learns mistakes are okay, and that he can take care of his own mistakes as a cooperative part of belonging in a group. He also learns that uncooperative behavior is not a reliable way to capture the teacher's attention.

The way we treat unintentionally uncooperative behavior—spills, accidental breakage, impulsive interrupting—can help determine whether the child will repeat that behavior in the future to achieve a feeling of belonging. As teachers, we can learn ways of reacting to children that encourage them to seek belonging through cooperative behavior.

The Four Goals of Misbehavior

Rudolf Dreikurs observed that children's misbehavior falls into four broad categories. Dreikurs called the categories *goals* because they represent ways children try to achieve belonging—even though their behavior is negative. The four goals of misbehavior are *attention, power, revenge,* and *display of inadequacy.*[3]

Attention. All children need and deserve attention. Giving infants and young children attention is part of our job as early childhood teachers. But attention can become a goal of misbehavior if children believe they can belong *only* when they are demanding and getting attention.

> *Four-year-old Juanita is excited about her painting and wants to share it with her teacher. She is asking for appropriate attention. The teacher recognizes how excited Juanita is by commenting, "It looks like you're having fun painting, Juanita. And you use such bright colors!" The teacher then moves on to work with other children, leaving Juanita happily absorbed in her painting.*

Juanita has asked for, and received, helpful attention. She feels she belongs because her efforts have been accepted. Attention would become a goal of misbehavior if Juanita believed and acted as if she were worthwhile *only* when she had the teacher's attention. In that case, Juanita might pursue the teacher to come see every time she put a new splash of paint on the paper.

> *"Look at my paper now . . . now look at this! Do you like it? Watch me paint some more. Did you see my new picture? Miss Coretta . . . watch!"*

This persistent behavior is a sign Juanita believes she belongs only while she holds her teacher's attention.

Power. Children want and seek power as well as attention. A positive sense of power gives children a feeling of *control* over

Sometimes children "misbehave" simply because they are curious, tired, sick, clumsy, trying to be helpful, or don't know the rules. In this case, the behavior we find troublesome isn't misbehavior at all. We may simply have unrealistic expectations.

their environment. It is an important step in gaining independence. But power becomes a goal of misbehavior when children believe they can belong only by being the boss. This kind of behavior can lead to a power struggle between the child and others.

> Two-year-old Brian throws temper tantrums when he doesn't get what he wants. The teacher scolds him and the tantrums get worse. At home, his mother gives in to the tantrums. Either way, Brian learns that temper pays off—he discovers that people either lose control or give in to him. Either way, he has the power he seeks!

Both teacher and parent could avoid reinforcing this kind of power-seeking misbehavior. They could refuse to be drawn in by Brian's tantrums and leave him to himself until he calms down. They could redirect his desire for power into positive channels by getting his assistance on projects and showing appreciation for his help when he gives it. (For a detailed discussion of temper tantrums, see Chapter 5.)

Revenge. Children prefer to get attention in pleasant ways. But if they aren't successful in gaining positive attention, they may misbehave to gain negative attention instead. If a child starts a power struggle to emphasize her need to belong and loses, the child is likely to feel hurt. As a result, the child may act on the third goal of misbehavior—revenge. When children seek revenge, it is because they believe they can belong only by hurting others as they feel they have been hurt.

Children generally misbehave for one of two reasons—because they are discouraged, or because their negative behavior is reinforced by those around them.

> Five-year-old Carol also throws tantrums. The teacher, Mrs. Thomas, refuses to involve herself in the tantrums or give in to the behavior. Carol strikes out, calling Mrs. Thomas names, and saying, "I hate you!" Mrs. Thomas feels hurt and angry. Carol has gotten her revenge.

Revenge is a sophisticated goal that doesn't generally occur until children move into the later toddler and preschool years. Although babies may learn to misbehave at times to gain attention or power as they get older, children that young usually don't misbehave to get revenge.

Display of inadequacy. The fourth goal of misbehavior is display of inadequacy. Like revenge, this goal is usually not seen in infants or toddlers. This is because displaying inadequacy is a response of children who have become completely discouraged over time in their search for belonging.

There are exceptions, such as children who have been abused. The issue of abuse is one that requires informed understanding by all adults who work with young children. See Appendix A for material on the subject of children and abuse.

Children who display inadequacy believe they can belong only when they convince others not to expect anything from them. They believe they are helpless. They give up, and convince those around them to do the same. Display of inadequacy usually results from months or years of discouragement about not finding a place through constructive means.

> *After a field trip to the zoo, the teacher provides paper and crayons so children can draw a picture of a favorite animal. Most of the children get busy coloring, but four-year-old Martin sits glumly staring at his blank paper. When his teacher approaches him, Martin exclaims, "I can't draw animals. They never look right!" Instead of trying to push Martin, the teacher suggests he draw a picture of anything he remembers about the trip. After a couple of minutes of sad looks, Martin picks up a crayon and draws a rectangle with lines in it. Taylor, who is sitting next to Martin, notices and says, "Teacher, come see Martin's cage!" The teacher acknowledges Martin's drawing and points out positive aspects of the picture. Although he doesn't smile, Martin does let out an audible sigh of relief.*

All children need and deserve attention. Attention becomes a goal of misbehavior when children believe they can only belong by demanding and getting attention.

Martin's teacher noticed his discouragement and avoided dwelling on an area where he felt inadequate. By suggesting he draw anything he remembered, she gave him permission to try something less threatening. If Martin believed he couldn't draw at all, the teacher might suggest an alternate activity such as modeling with clay or Play-Doh. If you were the teacher, your follow-up attention to whatever Martin produced would be especially important in situations like this.

Identifying the Goals of Misbehavior

How can teachers know when children are pursuing negative behavior goals? With infants, start with the assumption that the child is not misbehaving, but behaving normally out of a specific need. A cranky, crying baby may be bored, hungry, tired, or feeling sick. The child may need some gentle rocking or patting for comfort. While it's possible an older infant may begin to seek power and attention inappropriately, it's more likely during the first year of life that babies are simply using their natural communication ability to get their real needs met.

If you believe an infant's needs *are* being met, and troublesome behavior persists, then the child *may* be starting to pursue atten-

19

tion or power as a goal of misbehavior. It's easier to understand what's going on in the situation if you wait a while and observe the child's actions carefully before deciding what to do.

Identifying the Goal

With older children, it's easier to recognize true misbehavior and identify the goal. *The key to identifying a child's goals is found in your own response to the child's behavior.* To identify a child's goal, note carefully:

- *How you feel* when the misbehavior happens.

- *What you do* about the misbehavior.

- *How the child responds* to what you do about the misbehavior.

These three factors will help you determine the goal of the behavior.

(Later in this chapter we will discuss ways to respond to and redirect misbehavior.)

Attention. If a child has attention as his goal, you will probably feel annoyed by his behavior. You are likely to respond by reminding or coaxing the child to change the behavior. The child will likely stop the misbehavior—at least temporarily—because he received the desired attention. Later, the child may repeat the same act for more attention, or choose a different way to get your attention.

With infants, start with the assumption that the child is not <u>misbehaving</u>, but is behaving normally out of a specific need.

Four-year-old Jackson repeatedly interrupts the teacher during story time with questions and comments that are off the subject. The teacher tells him that "it's the teacher's time to talk." Jackson stops momentarily, then starts talking to the child sitting next to him.

Power. When a child is behaving in a way that seeks power, you will likely feel angry. You feel your authority has been challenged. You may try to make the child do what you want, or you may give in, figuring it's not worth a fight.

Two-and-a-half-year-old Alexandra pushes Josh out of the housekeeping corner and says, "Mine!" When you intervene and remind Alexandra about sharing, she throws a loud, escalating tantrum.

Toddlers are learning about ownership.

If you fight with a child in such a situation, you impress her with the value of power and she is likely to fight back. If you give in, she stops the misbehavior, because she has gotten what she was after. (See Chapter 5 for more information on handling temper tantrums.)

Revenge. A child who seeks revenge feels hurt and wants to get even.

> *Four-year-old Joe executes a karate kick that injures Carlotta. You step between the two children and restrain Joe, telling him, "I know you're angry, but I can't let you hurt Carlotta." Joe turns and punches you, saying, "I hate you! You're stupid! And you're ugly!"*

Your most likely response to a child's attempt at revenge is to feel emotionally hurt—and physically hurt if you've been attacked bodily. If you get angry and try to get even with the child, he is likely to respond by seeking more revenge. It is best to break the cycle of hurt and revenge by doing the unexpected. This will help the child redirect his behavior toward a more positive goal. (See the section on Doing the Unexpected for more information on this subject.)

Remember that infants don't usually pursue the goal of revenge. Toddlers do seek revenge at times. But their behavior can also

You and Your Relationships

Review your relationships with coworkers. Do you work together in an autocratic, permissive, or democratic atmosphere? If you identify personal differences in style that cause problems or confusion, you may want to raise the issue for discussion.

go out-of-bounds because they feel upset or overwhelmed. For example, biting does not necessarily indicate a goal of revenge—it could simply be an attempt to communicate frustration by a less verbal child.

Display of inadequacy. When a child displays inadequacy, you may feel like giving up. You may feel despair. Your response might be to take no action because you agree the child isn't capable and you don't expect her to perform the task. But achieving this kind of response is the purpose of the child's display of inadequacy to begin with. If you respond by giving up, the child will not improve.

> *Learning to share ideas and participate in a group has been difficult for four-year-old Jeremy. After numerous attempts to involve Jeremy, his teacher has begun feeling like giving up. Instead, Jeremy needs his teacher to continue finding ways of encouraging him to join in, a little at a time.*

More About Misbehavior Goals

Children are usually not consciously aware of the goals of their misbehavior. They often don't know they are after attention, power, revenge, or a display of inadequacy. They are, however, often aware of the consequences of the misbehavior. They learn what responses they get when they misbehave. Children can also change their goals depending on how they see a situation.

> *Three-year-old Craig clowns around at home to get attention. This gives him a sense of belonging. But at preschool with other children, Craig's clowning doesn't get him the attention he wants, so he begins to demand the teacher's attention more directly. He follows him around, interrupting him when he's with another child, pushing to be first. Craig's behavior at school is becoming a bid for power.*

One type of behavior may serve different goals. For example, a five-year-old who knows how to put on his coat passively waits for the teacher to help him when it's time to go home. This is attention-seeking behavior. Another five-year-old doesn't put on her coat—even though she's been taught how to do it—because she honestly believes she can't do it without help. This is a display of inadequacy.

Different kinds of behavior can also be used for the same goal.

When two-year-old Francesca doesn't want to come into the center when her father drops her off, she attempts to exert her power by crying. Later, when nap time comes, she shows her power by refusing to lie on her mat.

Display of inadequacy *always* involves passive behavior—because a child is discouraged, he does nothing. The other three goals *may* also involve passive behavior. For example, a child may seek attention passively, by simply expecting to be waited on, rather than actively, by shouting out at circle time. A child who stubbornly but silently refuses to budge when asked to come inside after outdoor time is taking a passive approach to pursuing power. Angry stares may indicate a wish for revenge.

Whether a child pursues a goal actively or passively, your clues to discovering the goal come from checking three things—your own feelings, the action you take, and the child's response to that action.

Redirecting Children's Behavior

Adults don't cause children to misbehave. Children make decisions about their own behavior based on the way they see things. However, adults reinforce a child's misbehavior goals by responding with behavior the child has come to expect.

Your clues to discovering a child's goal come from checking your own feelings, the action you take, and the child's response.

The best communication happens when you get down to the child's level.

If you respond the way a misbehaving child *expects* you to, you encourage the child to continue the misbehavior because it pays off. For example, if you respond by giving a child attention *every* time he wants it, even for positive behavior, he'll probably conclude that he belongs only when he is the center of attention. Then he will try to get you to stop whatever you're doing and pay attention to him frequently. If he doesn't get a pleasant response from you, he'll accept an unpleasant one—as long as he gets the attention he seeks.

Our goal as teachers is to help children develop positive behavior goals. This involves learning to respond to children in ways that do not reinforce misbehavior but serve to encourage movement in a positive direction.

Doing the Unexpected

The first step in redirecting a child's behavior is to do the unexpected.[4] If you do the opposite of what a misbehaving child expects, you won't reinforce the behavior. The child will get no payoff for the misbehavior. This may influence the child to change the behavior.

It is not always easy to do the unexpected. It means recognizing your feelings, and then changing your perspective and responding in a different way. This is a challenge that requires consistent effort for teachers. But it's important to make the effort, because children are sensitive to the genuine feelings underneath the things we say and do. Our reactions to children affect their learning and development. Knowing this makes the effort worthwhile.

The first step in redirecting a child's behavior is to do the unexpected.

In the five-year-old room, Jeff tells the teacher aide that Bethany used a swear word. The aide's first impulse is to scold Bethany. However, she realizes this choice would be giving attention to Jeff for tattling and to Bethany for swearing, reinforcing their goals of getting attention. She reminds herself that the long term goal is to reduce both tattling and swearing, and ignoring the behavior in each case may lessen it. So she simply nods and then redirects Jeff's attention to another part of the room instead of acting on the tattling. She also decides not to discuss the swearing with Bethany.

Encouraging Positive Behavior Goals

The second step in redirecting the child's behavior involves taking direct steps to encourage positive goals.

Attention. When possible, ignore misbehavior that seeks excessive attention. Refuse to be annoyed. Avoid always giving attention every time the child asks for it. And be sure to give positive attention at times when the child has *not* asked for it, and is not expecting it.

Three-year-old Emilio follows the teacher around asking a stream of questions. The teacher recognizes the questions are for the purpose of claiming her attention. She ignores Emilio and keeps moving. Later, the teacher deliberately looks for opportunities to give Emilio attention when he's not making a bid for it. When she sees him putting a puzzle together with another child, she says, "Emilio, I see you working with Margaret on the puzzle. It's nice to see you sharing."

Children who seek attention may also be seeking *involvement*. Encouraging such children to be helpful in group projects and to cooperate with others can help refocus the goal of getting attention in a way that is useful both to the child and to others.

Power. The best way to handle a power conflict is to withdraw from it by refusing *either* to fight or to give in—and by not letting yourself become angry. If possible, let the child experience the *consequences* of the misbehavior.

Four-year-old Stephanie tries to exert her power over the other children by hoarding all the blocks and refusing to share. Instead of challenging her bid for power by demanding she share, the teacher gives her a choice, "Blocks are for sharing. You can share the blocks or find something else to play with." Stephanie continues to hoard the blocks. The teacher respects her choice and simply takes Stephanie by the hand and leads her to another area of the room. Stephanie wails protests, which the teacher chooses to ignore.

Positive power means being responsible for one's own behavior and decisions. Redirect the power-seeking child by looking for ways to help the child build a positive sense of independence and capability.

Working with Parents
If you have a child with whom power struggles are a problem, set up a conference with the parents. Explain the principle of doing the opposite of what the child expects in the situation. Discuss with parents how they can help sidestep struggles they have with the child by helping the child use power positively at home.

> *Three-year-old Brady is quite verbal, but many of his comments involve negative interactions such as, "You can't make me!" Brady's teacher decides to enlist him as the attendance helper. Because Brady knows the names of all the children in his room, the teacher asks Brady to tell her who is present each day. Brady feels proud of his new job, and over time he begins to cooperate more often when his teacher asks him to get dressed or help clean up.*

Revenge. When a child is after revenge, it isn't easy to keep from feeling hurt. But the cycle of revenge can begin to subside when you understand the situation and work to avoid feeling hurt—difficult as it may be. Resist the temptation to get even. Work to build trust and respect.

Positive power means being responsible for one's own behavior and decisions. If you're involved in a power struggle with a child, look for ways to help the child build a positive sense of independence and capability.

> *Four-year-old Michiko becomes angry when, after adequate warning, the teacher tells her it's time to come inside because outside playtime is over. Michiko backs away, screaming, "I hate you! You're a creep!" The teacher says, "I know you don't want to come back inside. I like you very much, and I'm sorry you're unhappy. But outdoor time is over, and it's time for everybody to come back inside."*

The goal behind revenge behavior can be turned in a more useful direction. Seekers of revenge often have a strong desire for justice and fairness. Guiding such children to play and share equally encourages this.

Display of inadequacy. Remember that children who display inadequacy are extremely discouraged. It's important not to give up on such a child! Avoid criticism. Find *any* area of strength to encourage. Focus on the child's slightest effort or improvement.

> *Five-year-old Mario was discouraged because he could not cut as well as others in his group. After observing him struggle with the scissors—and finally give up—his teacher, Allen, suggested that he rip the construction paper strips into squares and glue them onto his paper. As he commented on the colorful paper scraps in Mario's collage, Allen made a mental note to locate a pair of adapted scissors and help Mario with some individual cutting practice at another time.*

Even aspects of a display of inadequacy can be refocused in a more positive direction. Displaying inadequacy involves withdrawal. Children can learn that sometimes it's courageous to withdraw from conflict or danger. This positive aspect of withdrawal can be noted and supported.

> **Remember . . .**
>
> It's important to keep in mind that troublesome behavior may or may not be "misbehavior." In dealing with children's behavior, consider each child's developmental level. Ask yourself whether she knows how to behave in a given situation, and is currently able to do so.
>
> Your efforts to redirect misbehavior will require lots of time and patience. Improvement won't come about overnight. Change is a gradual process. By being consistent and patient, you will eventually see results.

In the remainder of *Teaching and Leading Children*, we'll take a broader look at helpful ways to respond to children's misbehavior, and how to encourage positive goals.

Notes

1. Stella Chess and Alexander Thomas, *Know Your Child: An Authoritative Guide for Today's Parents* (New York: Basic Books, 1987), p. 13.

2. Sue Bredekamp (Ed.), *Developmentally Appropriate Practice in Early Childhood Programs Serving Children from Birth Through Age 8* (Washington, D.C.: National Association for the Education of Young Children, 1987), p. 31.

3. Rudolf Dreikurs and Vickie Soltz, *Children: The Challenge* (New York: Hawthorn Books, 1964), pp. 57-63.

4. Dreikurs and Soltz, p. 181.

Problem Situations

Infant. In the infant room, one-year-old Nikita's favorite plaything is a noisy push toy on wheels. She constantly wants to play with it, and cries and clings to it when other children try to take their turns using it. Every day there are several scenes in which the teacher tries to take the toy away, Nikita cries, and other children cry and try to take the toy as well.

1. Is Nikita behaving normally for her age and level of development, or is she misbehaving? Why?

2. What are some things the teacher can do to help Nikita and the other children in this situation?

Toddler. At naptime, two-and-a-half year old Mort has begun refusing to go to his cot. His teacher, Miranda, feels angry when Mort screams "No!" and runs to the block corner. She struggles with Mort all morning and looks forward to naptime as a chance to get a break from her battles with him. For the past three days, Miranda has had to carry Mort kicking and screaming out of the toddler room and leave him with an aide who plays blocks with him during naptime. By the end of the day, Mort is tired and cranky. And Miranda finds that she is having more struggles with Mort every day.

1. Is Mort misbehaving? If so, what do you think is his goal? Explain your answer.

2. What can Miranda do to stop reinforcing Mort's negative behavior? What are some more effective ways she might redirect Mort's behavior?

Preschooler. Lygia, who is five, appears unwilling to walk the balance beam on the playground. She enjoys the slide and the swings, and likes to run and play group games—but when her usual playmates line up for the balance beam, she stands back. Marco, who is playground aide during the preschoolers' outdoor time most afternoons, has noticed Lygia's hesitancy. He has been tempted to "cheer on" Lygia in an attempt to get her to try the beam, but he is afraid she may have trouble and doesn't want to set her up for failure.

1. Is Lygia displaying inadequacy? Explain your answer.

2. What can Marco do to deal with this situation?

Points to Remember

1. Each child is born with an individual temperament. Accept a child's temperament and work with it.

2. Each child goes through stages of development at his own individual rate and in his own particular style.

3. Children master new skills when they are ready.

   • Infants learn to trust other people, themselves, and the world around them.

   • Toddlers try independence.

   • Preschoolers create their own worlds, practice adult roles, play with language, and learn to get along with other children.

4. A democratic teacher-child relationship teaches children respect for self and others. It also builds responsibility by providing freedom within limits.

5. Teachers bring their expectations to their teaching. Children sense this, and do what is expected.

6. Find ways to say yes rather than no as often as possible.

7. Children discover they get a feeling of belonging from the responses of others. They learn they can get responses by either cooperative or uncooperative behavior.

8. Sometimes the fact that behavior troubles us is due to our inappropriate expectations of children. When children's actions stem from curiosity, tiredness, illness, hunger, boredom, or attempts to be helpful, they are not misbehavior.

9. In dealing with children's behavior, it is important to keep each child's developmental level in mind. It is also impor-tant to consider whether or not the child knows how to behave in a given situation and is able to do so.

10. There are four goals of misbehavior:

    • attention

    • power

    • revenge

    • display of inadequacy

11. To identify the goal of misbehavior, notice

    • how you feel when the child misbehaves.

    • what you do about it.

    • how the child responds to what you do.

12. Children usually are not aware of the goal of their misbehavior.

13. Troublesome behavior by infants is usually the result of specific needs rather than misbehavior. Babies can seek attention or power, but rarely revenge or display of inadequacy. Toddlers usually do not display inadequacy.

14. When a child misbehaves, do the opposite of what the child expects. Give positive attention and power. Work to build trust and self-confi-dence.

15. Four positive behavior goals we want to help children develop:

    • involvement

    • being responsible for one's own behavior and decisions

    • justice and fairness

    • courageously withdrawing from conflicts or dangerous situations

29

Child Development:

Note: This chart reflects the observations of several child development experts.* The "Qualities and Abilities" column lists positive qualities and describes what may be accomplished by the end of each period. However, every child is unique and may not match the chart. A child develops a skill when he or she is *ready*.

Age Range	What Child Is Learning	Qualities and Abilities
Birth to 3 months	Trust, cooperation, and personal power (such as the effects of crying)	Gains head control, grasps and holds, makes sounds. Smiles fully; smiles in response to human voices and contact. Shows distress, excitement, delight, boredom. Eats and sleeps in increasingly organized way.
3 to 6 months	To affect the environment through body movements	Sits supported. Rolls front to back to side. Has extended reach; grabs objects suddenly. Plays with fingers, hands, toes. Laughs when tickled, jiggled. Imitates sounds. Orally shows likes and dislikes. Recognizes familiar objects. Is very social.
6 to 9 months	More awareness of consequences of own behavior	Sits up, stands with assistance, crawls. Uses thumb and fingers to grasp small items. Explores objects by touching, feeling, shaking, banging, mouthing. Drinks from cup. Has depth perception. Becomes more independent—resists pressure. Imitates behavior. May say "Mama" and "Dada". May recognize own name and word **no**. Becoming aware of self as separate from others. Notices others' feelings, particularly other infants—joins them if they cry or laugh. Is anxious about strangers; may even be fearful of the familiar.
9 to 12 months	More awareness of consequences of behavior	Stands. Is better at grasping and holding. Drops objects but can't put something down intentionally. Often cooperates in getting dressed. May say a few words. Shows and recognizes moods. Is aware of nonverbal communication. Is often affectionate. Is more assertive. Gaining awareness of ownership—resists if toy is taken away. Is afraid of strangers and of separation from mother.
Ones	Beginnings of self-confidence	Walks (usually by 15th month). Explores; empties and fills things; drops and throws things. Feeds self. Follows simple directions. Plays alone for a short time. Imitates adult actions in play. Wants to be both independent and dependent. Uses clearer language. Names familiar objects. Becomes a toddler.
Twos	More self-confidence and mastery	Becomes more independent—wants to do things own way. At times, wants to return to babyhood.

Birth Through Age Five

Age Range	What Child Is Learning	Qualities and Abilities
		Navigates without bumping into things. Curious about everything—needs constant supervision. Speaks in 2- to 4-word sentences. Starts asking "what" and "why" questions. Has longer attention span and memory. Likes to help. Starts to play alongside other children. May offer to share a toy, but still gaining concept of "mine". Gets greater bowel and bladder control.
Threes	More sociability	Becomes more cooperative. Coordination greatly improves in gross and fine motor skills. Is talkative; enjoys hearing stories. Relates stories to familiar events. Asks for help when needed. Recognizes sex differences. Dresses self. Likes being with peers. Learns to take turns and share. May join simple group games and activities. Joins in dramatic play. May express fear of dark or monsters. Begins to understand ideas of yesterday, today, and tomorrow.
Fours	To refine previously learned abilities	Prefers children over adults. May have imaginary friends. Learning to cooperate in group activities. Prefers same-sex playmates. Is very active—runs, jumps, climbs. Fine motor abilities increase. Likes to talk, express ideas, and ask complicated questions. Tells stories, often exaggerating details. May show extreme mood changes, excited and then upset. Most have good bladder and bowel control, but may have accidents. Awareness of time grows.
Fives	To adapt to the world of childhood and formalized education	Begins to care about other children's opinions. Has more advanced reasoning powers. Has good control of hands and legs; eye-hand coordination is not fully developed—has accidents involving hands. Establishes handedness. Talkative, with good vocabulary. Appreciates humor; makes up own jokes. Likes to make friends. May have a best friend. Plays with both sexes. Develops a sense of fairness. Wants to be independent and to be treated as if grown up. Still needs comfort and encouragement from adults, but may not seek it.

* K. Eileen Allen and Lynn Morotz, *Developmental Profiles: Birth to Six*. (Albany, NY: Delmar, 1989) pp. 34-39, 42-47, 51-53, 62-64, 69-72, 81-84, 89-91, 97-98. T. Berry Brazelton, *To Listen to a Child: Understanding the Normal Problems of Growing Up* (Reading, MA: Addison-Wesley, 1984). pp. 157-65; Theresa Caplan and Frank Caplan, *The Early Childhood Years* (New York: Perigee Books, 1983), pp. 20-21, 122-23, 148-49, 172-73, 198-99, 232-33- 266-67; Fitzhugh Dodson and Ann Alexander, *Your Child: Birth to Age Six* (New York: Fireside, 1986), pp. 51-63, 179; Adrienne Popper, *Parents: Book for the Toddler Years* (New York: Ballantine Books, 1986), pp. 277-78; Benjamin Spock and Michael B. Rothenberg, *Dr. Spock's Baby and Child Care*, 40th. anniversary ed. (New York: Dutton, 1985), pp. 261-62, 286-87, 292-93, 307-9, 370-71, 376-77; Burton L. White, *The First Three Years of Life: The Revised Edition* (New York: Prentice Hall, 1985), pp. 161, 231-236.

Goals of Misbehavior

Note: With infants, start from the assumption that the child does not have a goal of *mis*behavior, but is behaving normally out of a specific need. The concept of *goals* has limited application to infants—usually only in the areas of attention and power. While it's possible that an older infant may seek attention or power through misbehavior, it's more likely during the first year of life that the infant is simply using communication skills she or he has to get real needs met. Babies usually do not pursue revenge or display inadequacy.

	Belief	Goal	Teacher's Reaction
Toddlers	I need to be noticed.	Attention	Annoyance. Tendency to remind child to stop.
	You can't make me.	Power	Anger, exasperation. Tendency to fight or give in.
	You don't love me!	Revenge	Deep hurt. Tendency to get even.
Preschoolers	I want to be noticed or served.	Attention	Annoyance. Tendency to remind child to stop.
	I am in control. You can't make me!	Power	Anger, exasperation. Tendency to fight or give in.
	You don't love me!	Revenge	Deep hurt. Tendency to get even.
	I am helpless. I can't.	Display of inadequacy	Despair, hopelessness. Tendency to agree with child that nothing can be done.

Toddlers are not likely to display inadequacy, because this goal comes after years of discouragement.

The following examples are just possibilities. The goal depends on how the teacher feels, what the teacher does, and how the child responds to the teacher's action.

Child's Response to Teacher's Reaction	Age Level Behavior	Alternatives for Teacher
Temporarily stops misbehavior. Later resumes behavior or disturbs in similar or other way.	Whines.	Give attention for positive behavior. Redirect child to more appropriate activity.
Intensifies misbehavior or submits with defiance.	Answers request for cooperation with immediate "NO!"	Give choices so child can make decision.
Seeks more revenge by intensifying misbehavior or choosing another weapon.	Hits or calls teacher names when doesn't get own way.	Avoid feeling emotionally hurt and punishing child. Build trust and mutual respect.
Temporarily stops misbehavior. Later resumes behavior or disturbs in similar or other way.	"Watch me now!" Seeks constant teacher contact.	Give attention for positive behavior when child is not making a bid for it. "Catch" child cooperating and comment.
Intensifies misbehavior or submits with defiance.	Has temper tantrums. Resists directions.	Withdraw from power struggle. Don't give in just to make peace. Let consequence occur.
Seeks more revenge by intensifying misbehavior or choosing another weapon.	Screams, yells, "You're mean! I hate you!"	Avoid feeling hurt and punishing child. Build trust and mutual respect.
Responds passively or fails to respond to whatever is done. Afraid to try and shows no improvement.	Whines, cries, "I can't do it!"	Encourage any efforts or attempts. Don't pity.

Applying Your Skills

When you encounter troublesome behavior with children, practice considering whether the behavior is the result of developmental factors or if it can be classified as misbehavior. You may decide to begin by focusing on the behavior of just one or two children.

If you decide a certain behavior is misbehavior, use the following steps to identify the goal.

- How do I feel when the child misbehaves in this way? What response does the child expect from me?

- What is my usual response?

- How does the child respond to what I usually do?

After you identify the child's goal, consider what changes you can make to redirect the misbehavior. Practice making the changes and consider the results. Remember, not all changes in children's behavior are immediate, but learning over time will probably yield positive results.

Things to Consider

While the skills we present have been found effective in most cases, you will want to determine a skill's effectiveness in your situation.

- Examine the child's environment—activities, materials, and scheduling factors that may be contributing to the troublesome behavior.

- Examine any personal liabilities on your part, such as being easy to anger, talking too much, being demanding, having to be in control, trying to be perfect, wanting to please.

- Assess your personal resources for solving this problem. These are qualities or strengths such as a sense of humor, the ability to step back and change mental gears, adeptness at problem solving, patience, or being perceptive.

Follow-Up

Your leader will provide time to discuss your results with the group at your next meeting. If your group does not meet again, plan a time to evaluate your efforts with others in your center who have taken the *TLC* class. If the results of the assignment are unsatisfactory, decide how you can modify your approach in the future.

Record Keeping (Optional)

You may find it helpful to log your observations and actions. The following format can be used for your log.

Daily Log   Child's Name:_____

	Behavior	My Response	Results
Monday			
Tuesday			
Wednesday			
Thursday			
Friday			

Just For You

Relieving Your Stress

Stress is a physical and emotional response to a demanding situation. Teaching young children is an intensive job. No wonder that stress builds up in the course of doing it every day. Here are several ways of easing and handling stress which may be helpful.

1. Use deep breathing for about fifteen seconds. Let your breathing pace itself. Silently, say "calm" as you breathe in, and "down" as you breathe out, until you begin to feel relaxed.

2. Use positive self-talk. Say simple, upbeat statements silently to yourself: "Be calm." "Take it easy." "You're okay."

3. Prepare yourself ahead of time for situations you think might be stressful. Take a few deep breaths and talk positively to yourself.

4. Think of situations as opportunities or challenges rather than as something stressful or something you're afraid you can't handle.

5. Every day, make it a point to accept yourself. Concentrate on your *own* positive qualities. Make self-affirming statements: "I'm capable." "I'm worthwhile." "I make my own decisions."

    Take a few moments now to jot down some affirming statements. Begin practicing stress reduction this week.

    To learn more about handling stress, read Edward Charlesworth and Ronald Nathan, *Stress Management* (New York: Atheneum, 1985).

Adapted from Don Dinkmeyer, Gary D. McKay, James S. Dinkmeyer, *Parenting Young Children* (Circle Pines MN: American Guidance Service, 1989) p. 21.

Chapter 2
Building Self-Esteem Through Encouragement and Listening Skills

What You Will Learn

- Encouraging children to believe in themselves and their abilities is an important part of your relationship with them.

- Praise is not as effective as encouragement.

- Encouragement involves having faith, providing hope, reducing competition, and eliminating high standards.

- Children need us to do a lot of listening. With reflective listening we help children understand and express feelings.

Building Self-Esteem in the Early Years

When children have strong self-esteem, it's easier for them to form positive beliefs about themselves and to find their places in the world. Self-esteem is a positive view of oneself. It's an attitude we develop when we are loved and we know we are capable. When we have healthy self-esteem, we have a positive self-image—we accept and value ourselves.

Children who feel good about themselves are better able to deal with the world. Self-esteem is the main factor that prepares a child to create successes and deal with failures.[1] Feelings of self-worth are beliefs that will form the basis of children's personalities and determine how they use their abilities. When children believe they are valuable, lovable, and worthwhile, they grow up ready to meet life's challenges.

Beginning at birth, the early childhood years are a critical period for developing self-esteem. During this time, children are forming beliefs about their own self-worth. They base their beliefs on the responses they get from others. It is a time when teachers and parents are in an excellent position to strengthen a child's sense of self-worth.

In this chapter, we will discuss mutual respect, encouragement, and reflective listening—important factors in helping children develop a healthy, positive view of themselves and their developing abilities.

Self-esteem is the main factor that prepares a child to create successes and deal with failures.

Mutual Respect—The Foundation of Self-Esteem

Learning mutual respect is the first step in developing self-esteem. Mutual respect means believing and behaving as if both adult and child are unconditionally valuable. You treat the children with respect. You expect them to treat you—and others—with respect.

Infants and young children do not naturally show respect for others. In fact, *it is normal and healthy for young children to be self-centered.* We can't expect them to be as respectful as adults can be. But young children are capable of *learning* mutual respect if they are treated respectfully.

It's never too early to begin sowing the seeds of mutual respect. To do this:

Appreciate children's uniqueness.

- "Look at what you can do!"

- "You really like to talk to yourself in the mirror. I like the way you pat the baby in the mirror gently."

Find ways to support their interests.

- "You like to build things. Let's make something in the block corner."

- "I know you like Curious George. Let's read the new book about him at story time."

Give them reasonable control over their lives when possible.

- "Would you like to choose red or green mittens from the mitten box?"

- "I can see you're tired of being in that swing. Would you like to get down and crawl around?"

Let them see that mistakes can be viewed as feedback, and are not to be feared.

- "I think we didn't put enough flour in this paste. See how runny it is? I think we'd better add some more so it will work better."

- "Oops, your glass of milk got knocked off the table. Next time, push it farther in from the edge. Let's get a towel and clean it up."

Teach them about cooperation—the ability to give and take in life. Make a human train to show that each part contributes to the whole. With older preschoolers, play a game without rules. Then play the game with rules. Discuss how they felt about both games.

Read stories that deal with mutual respect. You can also role play situations and see how children respond to respect and disrespect. Have the children role play a situation where someone takes unfair advantage of others. Ask the children how they feel in the situation.

Remember to show respect for yourself.

- "I had a nice long walk on the way to the center—that helped me feel good today!"

- "When you shout, my ears hurt. I'll be glad to listen if you talk in a quieter voice."

Encouragement—The Key Ingredient

Mutual respect provides the foundation for children's self-respect. Teachers can use the skill of encouragement to help build on this foundation.

- *Respect is an attitude* we can model and teach.

- *Encouragement is a skill* we can learn to use to help children grow in self-esteem.

Encouragement is a basic human need. Helping children believe in themselves and in their abilities is an important part of your relationship with them.

Encouragement involves having faith, providing hope, reducing competition, and eliminating high standards. It helps children develop positive attitudes and beliefs about themselves by focusing on their strengths and assets.[2] When we encourage children, we accept them, even though we don't always accept their behavior.

- "I can see that you were wanting to be helpful when the plates dropped."

It is never too early to begin sowing the seeds of mutual respect.

39

With encouragement, we recognize effort and improvement— rather than expecting or demanding perfection. Teachers help each child appreciate his or her own unique, individual qualities.

With encouragement, we recognize effort and improvement— rather than expecting or demanding perfection. Teachers who encourage avoid comparing children. Comparisons can lead children to believe their worth depends on being better than others. With encouragement, teachers help each child appreciate his or her own unique, individual qualities.

When children don't receive encouragement, they are likely to become discouraged. Discouragement grows out of the belief that one is not adequate to meet life's challenges.[3] Discouraged children lack confidence in their ability to accomplish tasks. They are literally dis-couraged. They focus more on their success than on their effort. Fearing they may not do well, discouraged children may even avoid the task altogether.

A discouraged child often says, "I can't." This can result in the child trying to get others to do things for him. As children grow older, they will take less responsibility for their actions if they continue to lack courage. Children who *believe* in themselves are excited about life and learning.

Encouragement Skills

Children's ability to learn is related to their self-concept and expectations for themselves.[4] Discouraged children who believe themselves to be poor learners perform according to their negative expectations. Encouragement helps the child overcome these negative expectations by focusing on assets, resources, and efforts.

Teachers who encourage help children believe in themselves and what they can do. They help the children find ways to handle challenges. When you encourage children regularly, you show confidence in them and in yourself.

Encouragement can be learned. Here are some skills of encouragement:

Accept and value children as they are. Children learn at different rates and have different abilities and interests. Their moods and behaviors have ups and downs. Each child has individual strengths and weaknesses. By recognizing and appreciating the differences between people, teachers show children they are valued just as they are.[5]

Show you believe in children.

- "I know you can put that puzzle together."

- "Go ahead—you can reach the ball by yourself."

Let them know it's important to keep trying. Tell them it's okay to make mistakes because mistakes are an important part of learning. Encourage persistent effort rather than focusing on results. Often children's feelings of confidence come from the spark you provide by letting them know you believe in them. Learn to appreciate small successes and gradual growth.

Treat all children with respect. You're human, so there will be some children who are favorites. It's important to recognize you may tend to favor some children. Make an effort to treat *each* child with equal respect. The encouraging classroom demands that everyone be treated equally. Double standards can be devastating.

Help children value their own worth. Make it clear their worth doesn't depend on being better than others. Judgments and comparisons are not encouraging. Encouraged children believe in their own value. Help children learn to cooperate rather than compete. Pitting children against each other makes winning more important than learning or cooperation.

Appreciate children's strengths and positive qualities.

- "Look at the way you are sharing your toys today!"

- "Just look at what you are able to do all by yourself!"

- "Thank you. That was very helpful."

- "I appreciate it when you _____ because it makes my job much easier."

- "I needed your help and you can be counted on. "

- "I really enjoyed having you here today."

- "It's really thoughtful when you _____."

Use your sense of humor. See things in perspective: "Goodness! I must look silly with my art smock inside out!" Keeping a sense of humor helps children see that mistakes are feedback for learning. Both you and the children can relax when mistakes occur. Humor is also a great self-encourager!

The Difference Between Encouragement and Praise

In their efforts to build children's self-esteem, teachers sometimes confuse encouragement with praise. But praise and encouragement are *not* the same thing. Each has a different purpose and effect.

Praise is a type of verbal reward. It is based on competition and comparison. When children hear praise, the message often received is, "When you do something that I think is praiseworthy,

Working with Parents
Write a note to parents about using feeling words when they talk with their children. You may want to list some of the feeling words from this chapter.

then you are valued." Praise is an external motivator. It is given when the child has accomplished something, completed a task, or pleased the teacher.

Encouragement is given for effort or improvement. It isn't based on competition or comparison, but on the child's assets and strengths. Encouragement from teachers helps children learn to accept themselves and feel worthy and valued as they are. The message the child receives is, "I don't have to be *more* to feel good about myself. I am good enough as I am."[6]

Imagine your children are running a race. Whatever is said or done when they cross the finish line is praise. Whatever is said or done while they run the race is encouragement. Encouragement focuses on the effort, on enjoying the process, rather than the result. For most children, it feels as though they are always racing in competition with themselves and others. Children need continuous encouragement along the way.

Encouragement supports a child's self-esteem. It can be given at any time, even when the child feels discouraged or faces a failure. Encouragement recognizes effort and contributions. It helps children learn the value of being useful by contributing. Encouragement is an internal motivator and builds the child's self-esteem.

Praise and encouragement are not the same thing. Encouragement helps a child become self-motivated. Praise teaches a child to please others.

In the course of a day there are many opportunities to offer encouragement.

> *The teacher is walking around the room observing chil-dren's activities. The teacher isn't exactly sure what it is that four-year-old Nikki has made. She says to Nikki, "Wow! Fantastic job! I am so proud of you!"*

Nikki may be pleased with the way the teacher is responding to her project. But Nikki is also learning that it is important to please others. If she continues to only hear praise for the results of things she does, she may begin to believe what others think of her determines her worth. She might be afraid of the times she doesn't hear her teacher praise the things she does.

> *Three-year-old Sam brings the teacher a drawing he made. The teacher says to Sam, "I can see you're really happy with your drawing. I noticed you like to use a lot of different col-ors."*

In this example, the teacher encourages Sam to appreciate his own efforts. He wants Sam to learn to make his own judgments rather than deciding on the basis of the teacher's opinion if he is worthy. The teacher could also ask Sam, "What else can you tell me about your picture?"

Encouragement helps a child become self-motivated. Praise teaches a child to please others. There is nothing wrong with wanting to help and please someone. The problem is when the child believes that pleasing others is a *must* in order to feel good about herself. At times we may want to use praise. When we do, it is important to use it *with* encouragement for the purpose of encouraging the child.

> *Two-and-a-half year old Jolie has been having difficulty separating from her mother when she is dropped off in the morning. Usually she has a tantrum and cries through the morning. Today, however, Jolie makes the transition with a minimum of crying and a few quick sniffles. The teacher, Mr. Wylie, responds, "Great job Jolie! I see you are ready to start playing right away today. What would you like to play with first?"*

Jolie may not even recognize that she is controlling this behav-ior better, or that this is an accomplishment. The teacher's en-couraging words give her that information. If Jolie cries again the next day, the teacher doesn't make an issue of it. Instead, he helps Jolie gain control of the situation by focusing on things she can do in the room.

Repeated encouragement over days and weeks will help Jolie make the successful transition of being separated from her mother. The teacher's encouraging words and praise are valuable to Jolie because she is accepted and loved regardless of how she acts when her mother leaves.

(See Chart 2 at the end of the chapter on the difference between encouragement and pressure.)

Encouragement is not always verbal. An accepting attitude, a willingness to let children try things on their own, and the acceptance of mistakes are all important ways of encouraging children.

The Language of Encouragement

Because praise can be overdone, teachers will be most effective if they don't praise children *too* often. Encouragement has a more lasting effect because it helps children believe in themselves. Encouragement notices effort and improvement rather than focusing on results.

Here are some phrases that use the language of encouragement:

- "You really enjoy doing that."
- "You feel happy!"
- "How do you feel about it?"
- "You can do it."
- "Thanks. That helped me a lot."
- "I need your help on _____."
- "You really worked hard on that!"
- "You're getting better at _____." (Be specific.)
- "It was thoughtful of you to _____."
- "Your hard work helped all of us."
- (To the group) "I really enjoyed today. Thank you."

Encouraging Learning

We want to encourage children to learn, but without pushing them. We want to follow and support their individual interests.

Some adults believe children need to be prepared as early as possible so they will be high achievers in academics and athletics. When teachers push children hard and fast, children pay a price. They may not be developmentally ready for the tasks they are asked to undertake. When children aren't ready or interested, they may become discouraged and begin to make negative bids for attention or power. Some may even seek revenge, or begin to display inadequacy. (See Chapter 1 for more information on negative behavior goals.)

Noted early childhood authorities like Burton White and David Elkind point out the dangers of pressuring children.[7] The approximate times when most children learn various skills have been studied and documented. Physical, psychological, emotional, intellectual, and social readiness are very important to learning. Trying to speed up the learning process by pressuring children can result in short and long term effects. These may include anxiety, stomach and headaches, and rebellion. In later years, the consequences can lead to alcohol and other drug abuse—and in the extreme—suicide.

Learning is supported when teachers understand the typical skills children acquire at certain periods in their lives. Teachers need an encouraging attitude toward children's attempts to learn and discover. A teacher's positive relationships with both parents and children are also an important part of guiding young children. (See Chapter 6 for more information on working with parents.)

Encouraging learning involves discovering what the child can do. Then, a teacher can provide materials and plan activities to enhance the child's stage of development, rather than push it. We encourage learning by setting reasonable goals children are ready to achieve, accepting children's efforts, and appreciating improvements.

Encouragement is not always verbal. An accepting attitude, a willingness to let children try things on their own, and the acceptance of mistakes are all important ways of encouraging children.

Two-year-old Shauna is learning to use the potty, with a lot of encouragement in the toddler room and at home. When she gets through her first full afternoon of using the toilet with no accidents at the preschool, her teacher relays the news to her father when he picks her up. Shauna's father says, "Good for you, Shauna! I bet you're proud of yourself." Shauna beams happily. She feels good inside because both her teacher and her parent notice her efforts and strides in toilet training and comment on them.

Earlier on, when Shauna was wetting her pants more often, no one made a big issue of it. Instead, her teacher said, "Looks like you need some dry pants. Why don't we go to the bathroom so you can get cleaned up and be more comfortable."

As a teacher, you want your children to learn how to face challenges and changes. You want them to develop skills and a positive attitude toward learning. Your children will fare better in life if you are more interested in *how they learn to learn* rather than how they perform. Focus more on their efforts rather than on results.

Your children will fare better in life if you are more interested in <u>how they learn to learn</u> rather than how they perform. Focus more on their efforts than on results.

- "You've almost got that shoe on. Keep pushing—your heel will fit in."

- "Look at you feeding yourself applesauce!"

- "How could we make these bead necklaces the same length?"

Here are some guidelines for how to encourage children to learn without using praise or pressure:

1. **Provide a developmentally appropriate environment which encourages learning experiences.** Allow students plenty of opportunities to explore and play with other children.
   - "How many bean bags can you throw into this laundry basket?"
   - "The baby dolls need a bath. How much soap should we put in the tub?"
   - "How high can you climb on the monkey bars?"
   - "How high should we build the tunnel so the truck can fit under?"
   - "How can we use these rubber bands to make shapes on the pegboard?"
   - "Banging pots and pans makes a lot of noise. What happens when we bang on the carpet?"

2. **Follow each child's interest.** Discover each child's interests and help each discover new ones. For instance, if children like animals, find books or cassette stories about them. Help children create stories about animals.
   - "You like scrunching those papers. Here's some soft tissue paper to scrunch."
   - "I've been watching you walk on the balance beam. Could we play follow the leader, and I'll copy you?"

3. **De-emphasize competition.** You may unintentionally communicate verbal or nonverbal comparisons between students. Recognize that children learn and develop at different rates. Overemphasizing competition creates discouraged children. Show the children you appreciate them just the way they are:
   - "I'm so glad you're in my group."
   - "I liked sitting by you and reading that story. You seemed so interested!"
   - "I can tell you're scared of the thunder. It feels good to hold someone's hand when you're frightened."
   - "Look at that shiny new tooth. What a grin!"

4. **Ask open-ended questions.** When you ask a yes or no question, the child is not required to think, explain, and explore. Instead of saying, "Did you have a good day today?" ask, "What things did you do today that you enjoyed?"

Other examples of open-ended questions and phrases:
- "How did you make your clay snake so long?"
- "Please tell me how you built this box sculpture."

5. **Notice any small efforts.**
- "You've almost got that zipper done. Keep pulling and it will go the rest of the way up."
- "Look at what you can do all by yourself!"

6. **Make learning fun.** Make games out of learning. With the children, count how many people are here today, or how many snacks to put out. Compare how many children are swinging or sliding at any given time. Teach feelings by having children guess what you are feeling when you make a face. Or act out stories about characters with a variety of feelings.

It is important to recognize that children are learning when they play. Many of us assume children are just passing time when they're playing. However, play allows children to discover new behaviors. It helps them learn more about how others respond to them. Finding a regular time to play *with* children is just as important as allowing them to play with their peers. Seeing adults enjoy themselves lets children know it is okay to have fun.

The teacher is teaching her toddler group how to play "Ring Around the Rosie." When she gets to "All fall down!" the teacher collapses on the floor laughing. The toddlers imitate her by falling down in a jumble.

The preschool room has a doctor's office set up in the dramatic play center. The teacher comes moaning and limping. He says, "I think I hurt my leg. Is there anybody here who could fix it?" After being bandaged and receiving multiple pretend shots, he says, "Thank you. I'm feeling much better now."

---

7. **Help children see the alternatives in challenging situations.** One way to do this is to break overwhelming tasks into smaller pieces.
   - "It looks like there are a lot of things to pick up. What could you start with first?"
   - "That was fast. Now what can you pick up next?"

8. **Help children have the courage to be imperfect.** Children need to know that the process of mastering skills is progressive. It's natural and accepted that sometimes their efforts will not be fully successful. Children develop the courage to be imperfect when they come to understand that mistakes are a part of learning.

In order to respect children you need to respect yourself.

Five-year-old Doug is trying hard to master hammering nails at the workbench. The nails keep bending over, or the wood splits. Doug's teacher comes over and says, "Doug, you're trying very hard. Let me show you a trick for keeping the nails straight. There, you'll get it if you keep practicing."

Two-year-old Carmen is trying to dress herself. She tries to tug her shirt over her head and grunts in frustration when it won't pull down. Her teacher says, "Carmen, I see you're learning how to get dressed. Turtleneck shirts are hard."

When you find yourself feeling overwhelmed, it's time for a little self-encouragement.

The Courage to Be Imperfect[8]

Helping children learn it's okay to be imperfect is an important part of building their self-esteem. Children with the courage to be imperfect are willing to take healthy risks and learn. They have an "I'll try," rather than a "Why try?" attitude. The same thing is true for adults. As you think about the challenges of building your children's self-esteem, learning to encourage, and teaching them basic skills, it's easy to feel overwhelmed and discouraged yourself. Your first thought may be, "How can I possibly be successful at all of this? What if I make a mistake?"

It may help if you remind yourself you can't always show respect or be a constant model of encouragement. You're human. What you can do is keep in mind a general attitude of mutual respect, make an effort to encourage as much as you can—and have the courage to be imperfect.

When you develop the courage to be imperfect, you accept yourself and others as they are, without the need to focus on mistakes or imperfections. You do not fear mistakes. If you have the courage to be imperfect, you concentrate on the present instead of worrying about the past or future. Most of our discussion has been on how to develop children's self-esteem. But it's also very important for teachers themselves to have strong self-esteem. In order to respect children you need to respect yourself. There are a number of ways to build and maintain your own self-esteem and self-respect. It will be helpful if you work to:

- Develop your own interests and goals.

- Recognize efforts, rather than focusing only on results.

- Be positive about yourself and others.

- Use your sense of humor to keep things in perspective.

- Realize that you'll make mistakes, but that the children in your care will learn and grow anyway.

- Remember you are worthwhile just as you are, simply because you are human. Your worth is not dependent upon pleasing children and parents.

Working with children is a challenging task. Neither you or your children will always handle behavior and emotions "correctly." You need to encourage yourself. Recognize what you are doing well. Focus on what helps you feel good about yourself. Above all, work to develop the courage to be imperfect.

Courageous teachers:

- See challenges rather than problems.

- Get satisfaction from doing their best, not from outside evaluation or from results.

- Consider what to do in a difficult situation, rather than see it as just hopeless.

- Accept that they will make mistakes—there are no "perfect" teachers.

- Believe their possibilities for success are greater if they keep trying.

Teachers with strong self-esteem help children develop strong self-esteem. Children who see their teachers role model facing life's challenges with courage are better prepared to develop the courage to do the same.

Listening to Children

In working and playing with children, we want to build both mutual respect and self-respect. One important way to foster these is by learning to listen carefully to children's feelings.

Listening Skills

Children need us to do a lot of listening. If we listen well, we can help them identify, accept, and understand their feelings. We help them discover positive ways to deal with feelings and problems. And we encourage them to become effective listeners as well.

Talking is one way people communicate, but it's not the only way. Our body language and tone of voice often say more than the words we use. This is especially true with young children. They often don't have the words to communicate their feelings and wants. We have to watch their body language—their facial expressions and body movements—to find out what children are trying to tell us.

Teachers with strong self-esteem help their children develop strong self-esteem.

> *Eighteen-month-old Norma scowls and pounds the shapes on the shape sorter, trying to force the round shape into the square hole. Norma's teacher Jim comes over and says, "I can see you feel angry because it won't fit. Let's look for another hole it might fit into."*

We also need to be aware of what our body language and tone of voice communicate to children. Our actions show children whether or not we understand and respect them.

> *Eleven-month-old Meduka has been repeatedly trying to pull himself to a stand against the side of his crib. Meduka keeps wobbling and falling down. On the third attempt he bangs his head on a crib bar and starts crying. His teacher picks him up and hugs him. Then she says, "I bet that hurt. You've been trying hard to stand up, and it's no fun to keep falling over."*

Children may not clearly state what they need to have understood. A complex message usually deals with a child's *feelings* about a situation—what the situation means to her. The child wants the meaning heard, understood, and accepted.

This is what we want for ourselves, too. Picture the following situation.

> *A neighbor's pet rabbit destroyed your prized flower garden. You tell a friend, "My whole garden is ruined! Nothing's left." Your friend says, "Well, what's done is done. Forget it and start over. Anyway, you think you've got problems? You should hear what happened to me yesterday."*

The friend's response shows she knows your garden is ruined, yet she gives no recognition of your feelings about the situation. She shows no *respect* for your feelings.

You want your feelings to be heard, understood, and accepted. When they are, you believe your feelings are important and worthy of attention. You receive a message of care and concern. That invites you to offer care and concern for the feelings of others. The same is true of children. They want to be fully heard too.

The way you listen to and express feelings models a skill for children to develop. Working with young children gives you plenty of opportunities to model effective listening skills. From the start, teachers who work with infants can respond effectively to babies' communication. Effective listeners learn to understand the communications in infants' cry and body language. A cry may say a child is hungry, tired, wet, bored, scared, or angry. We need to tune into body language. Infants may tell us they are happy by smiling. They might tell us they are angry or impatient by twisting away while being dressed.

As they grow, babies learn which signals will get them picked up. Sometime after their first year, most children begin to speak in words. Later, words become full sentences. But even then, children's meanings and feelings are often not clearly stated in words. Yet children need to be understood.

Young children find it difficult to see things from someone else's perspective. (Remember, children under five or six are naturally self-centered.) But as they come to know their feelings are valued, they gradually gain an understanding of others' feelings and the importance of listening.

Reflective Listening

We recommend using *reflective listening* to encourage children to be aware of and trust their own feelings, and to express their feelings constructively. With reflective listening you *reflect*, like a mirror, the feelings the child expresses. Reflecting his feelings first helps a child feel understood. Later on, it helps the child learn the language of feelings and to express feelings more clearly.

Reflective listening is a skill. It's also an attitude—it means letting children know you value what they feel and what they say. Reflective listening means being open to the meaning behind children's words and body language. It means *wanting to understand*, and communicating that fact clearly to the children in the responses you make to them.

Our body language and tone of voice often say more than the words we use.

As a skill, reflective listening is done as follows:

1. **Establish eye contact.** Let your body position show that you are listening. If a child's eye level is at your knee or your waist, this may mean bending or kneeling down to the child's height. You could also pick the child up, or you can both sit down.

2. **Hear and define the feeling.** After listening with full attention, ask yourself, "What's she feeling?" Make a guess. Then think of a word that describes that feeling.

3. **State the feeling.** Now use the feeling word in a sentence. (See Words for Feelings later in this chapter for some feeling words.)

Many teachers find it easier to start with a formula for reflective listening:

"You feel (state the feeling) because (state the reason behind the feeling.)"

- "You feel sorry because Mickey got hurt."

- "You feel excited because your bottle is ready."

- "You feel angry because Joey took the blocks."

Once you have the "You feel_____ because _____" formula firmly in mind, you may want to use less structured statements:

- "You're sorry because Mickey got hurt."
- "You're so excited to see your bottle."
- "You're really mad at Joey for taking the blocks."

Reflecting feelings this way lets children know you have heard the feelings and meanings behind the words. Like a mirror, you reflect what you see or hear children say.

Words for Feelings

It's important to begin early to give children a vocabulary of feeling words. In their first two years, children learn a great deal of language. Along with the words for cup and ball, they need to hear words for their feelings—words like happy, sad, mad. As children grow older, they can learn more specific words for feelings. Knowing words for feelings encourages a child's self-understanding and self-acceptance. If she has the words, a child can talk about her feelings. When you reflect children's feelings by using accurate feeling words, they learn to identify and describe their feelings.

Sometimes you may find it challenging to think of words to explain feelings. Here are some examples of feeling words:

angry	sad	great	mad
confused	scared	better	happy
disappointed	sorry	enjoy	like
frightened	unfair	excited	worried
hate	unhappy	glad	pleased
hurt	good	proud	left out

(Note: Using the word "upset" often communicates that you don't really understand. It's best to be more specific.)

> *Three-year-old Matt comes whimpering to the teacher, complaining that Jay took the dinosaur away from him. The teacher says, "You're really sad because Jay took the dinosaur." (The teacher could then call the two boys together and suggest they talk about it. See Chapter 3 for a discussion of problem solving.)*

At times, you won't be sure what a child is feeling. It's okay to make a guess.

> *Four-year-old Pablo tells his teacher, "My dad is mean! He won't let me do anything." His teacher isn't sure what Pablo means, so she responds, "It sounds like you're really angry with your dad. Do you want to tell me what happened?"*

As long as they sense your sincere interest, children will usually redirect you if you've misinterpreted the feeling.

When adults use reflective listening with children, the children get information about their feelings. Their teacher talks about the feelings—she or he doesn't attack, but shows understanding. The children learn it must be okay to have and show emotions.

When Is It Appropriate to Use Reflective Listening?

Reflective listening can be helpful when a child is showing strong emotion. A child may use body language (crying, hitting, going rigid, laughing, hugging), or strong words ("I hate you!" "I want to go home!").

It's also appropriate to use reflective listening when no emotion is apparent, but you realize a child's feelings are below the surface.

> *It's four-year-old Leah's first day at your preschool. She stands with her mother—reluctant to join in learning center activities. You sense she may be afraid. You approach her and say, "You look kinda scared—maybe because you don't know some of the children." Leah nods. You offer to take her hand and introduce her. She looks at her mother. Mom smiles and indicates it's okay. Leah takes your hand and goes with you toward a group of children.*

When you have to deny a child's request, reflective listening helps soften the "no" response: "You're angry because I won't read you another book, but it's time for music."[9] Don't let the

Reflective listening lets your child know you have heard the feeling and meaning behind the words. Like a mirror, you reflect what you see or hear him saying.

child drag you into an argument: "I know you're mad, but the answer is still no. I'm going to start music time now."

Children's feelings need to be understood and respected. However, teachers shouldn't accept verbal abuse. If a child calls you a name, recognize his anger, but let him know you won't accept insults: "I can hear that you're very angry with me. That's okay—you can say, 'I'm angry with you, Mrs. Brown.' But I won't listen to you when you call me names." Once you explain your limits, ignore the child if he keeps calling you names. If he continues, focus your attention on other children.

Reflective listening isn't always necessary. Most of the time, children's messages are clear and simple. When a child simply says, "I want to play with the blocks," there is usually no hidden meaning in the words.

It's natural for young children to think they are the center of the world and to expect to be listened to constantly. But this is neither possible nor desirable. You have many children to relate to—you can't pay constant attention to any one of them. It's a challenge to show children both that we want to hear what they have to say, and that there are limits on our time to listen. If you don't have time at a given moment to listen, say so. Tell the child he can talk to you later.

Reflective listening is a skill. It's also an attitude—it means letting children know you value what they feel and what they say.

Babies won't understand all our words, but they will sense our interest and caring.

- "I can see that you're excited about your picture. After George and Sue tell me their stories, I'll be glad to hear you tell me about it."

When to Begin Using Reflective Listening

We believe it makes sense to use reflective listening with even the youngest infants. Very young children will miss the meaning of the words, but they will not miss the supportive attitude shown in teachers' voices and faces.

- "I see you like your teddy bear."

- "Oh, you reached for the rattle!"

- "If you open your mouth, the food will go in easier. And you won't feel so mad and hungry . . . There you go!"

Using reflective listening helps establish an atmosphere of mutual respect between teachers and infants and toddlers. Along with understanding and respect for others, it's an important first step in developing self-esteem.

Notes

1. Dorothy Corkille Briggs, *Your Child's Self-Esteem: The Key to Life* (New York: Doubleday, Dolphin Books, 1975), p. 3.

2. Don Dinkmeyer and Lewis Loconcy, *The Encouragement Book: Becoming a Positive Person* (Englewood Cliffs, NJ: Prentice Hall, 1980), p. 65.

3. Gary McKay, *The Basics of Encouragement* (Coral Springs, FL: CMTI Press, 1976), p. 3.

4. William Purkey, *Self-Concept and School Achievement* (Englewood Cliffs, NJ: Prentice Hall, 1980).

5. Don Dinkmeyer, *The Basics of Self-Acceptance* (Coral Springs, FL: CMTI Press, 1992).

6. Dinkmeyer, *The Basics of Self-Acceptance*

7. David Elkind, *The Hurried Child* (Addison-Wesley, 1981) and Burton White, *The First Three Years of Life* rev. ed. (New York: Prentice Hall, 1985).

8. The concept of "The Courage To Be Imperfect" was originally developed by Dr. Rudolf Dreikurs, an internationally known author and psychiatrist.

9. Stanley Greenspan and Nancy Thorndike Greenspan, *First Feelings* (New York: Viking Penguin, 1985), p. 211.

Problem Situations

Infant. Eight-month-old Corey seems to want his teachers and the older children to give him the toys he wants, rather than crawl to them to get them himself. Even though Corey can crawl, he often lies on his stomach and cries as he reaches toward a ball or rattle. To help keep peace, Corey's teacher, Mrs. Yakov, gives Corey the toys he cries for. This only helps for a short time though—soon Corey is crying for something else just out of reach.

1. What might be the goal of Corey's crying?

2. In what ways might Mrs. Yakov's response to Corey's behavior be discouraging Corey? Should Mrs. Yakov be giving Corey a chance to crawl and get the toys he wants?

3. How might Mrs. Yakov use reflective listening and encouragement to help Corey learn to help himself get the toys he wants?

Toddler. Lately, two-and-a-half-year-old Ellie has cried and clung to her father when he drops her off at the center early in the morning. Her wails are so heartbreaking that Ellie's father and her teacher have begun to promise Ellie special treats, and special treatment, to get her mind off her dad's leaving. This morning, Ellie's father told her, "Ellie, I promise I'll bring you a cookie after work today if you don't cry. And I bet Ms. Napoli will read you the Mickey book as soon as I leave." Ms. Napoli agreed, and Ellie ran to get the book. But the aide was late, and breakfast had to be served, so Ms. Napoli told Ellie she'd have to wait to read her the story. Ellie burst out crying and screamed, "I want Mickey! I want my daddy! I want cookie!" and began crying inconsolably. Ms. Napoli felt angry and frustrated. As she brought out breakfast and greeted other parents and children for the morning, she gritted her teeth and carried a screaming Ellie in her arms.

1. Is Ellie misbehaving? If so, what might the goal be? How are Ellie's Dad and Ms. Napoli discouraging Ellie?

2. How could Ms. Napoli use reflective listening right now to let Ellie know her feelings are being understood?

3. What are some ways Ms. Napoli could respond differently on future mornings in order to encourage Ellie and help establish a smoother transition time?

Preschooler. All through the day, four-year-old Brian makes loud and sometimes aggressive bids for the teacher's notice. During circle time, he interrupts to talk about himself. He always waves his arm as hard as he can to be called on. On the playground, he hollers for the teacher to watch what he's doing and to join in his play. At naptime, he calls the teacher to his cot again and again. If the teacher is talking with another child about an art project, Brian will push the child aside to get next to the teacher and say, "You like my picture better, don't you?" If the teacher is with a group of children putting together a block tower, Brian will step between the teacher and the children and say, "Did you see the tower I built?"

1. What might be the goal of Brian's misbehavior? How might Brian's teacher respond so as not to give in to constant bids for attention?

2. What are some ways Brian's teacher might encourage Brian so he will feel better about himself and less needy of attention?

Chart 2

Encouragement vs. Pressure

	Encouragement	Pressure
Infants	Allowing infant to explore surroundings at own pace.	Overstimulating or forcing a challenge infant not ready for. Introducing infant to animal when clearly afraid.
	Giving infant age-appropriate toys.	Giving infant toys beyond age or ability level.
	Allowing infant to develop at own physical rate.	Coaxing infant to crawl or walk before physically capable.
	Helping infant give up bottle when she shows interest in using cup.	Forcing infant to give up bottle before ready.
Toddlers	Supporting toddler in beginning toilet training when he shows interest and physical ability to control bodily functions.	Forcing toddler to use potty or begin toilet training before he shows interest or is physically capable.
	Helping toddler give up pacifier, blanket, or security object when he shows interest in doing so.	Removing security object when child is still emotionally dependent on it.
	Guiding toddler to display age-appropriate behavior, such as trying to use eating utensils in social situations.	Demanding that toddler behave more maturely.
Preschoolers	Encouraging learning of age-appropriate skills.	Trying to teach concepts beyond preschooler's understanding.
	Setting stage for creative, spontaneous play.	Demanding rigid, structured play format.
	Encouraging preschooler to try not to be afraid of mistakes. Encouraging risk taking.	Stressing doing things "right." Discouraging any efforts unless done perfectly.

Applying Your Skills

This week practice encouragement with the children in your center. You may decide to begin with just one or two children.

Remember, encouragement involves focusing on efforts, strengths, showing faith, and using communication skills.

Things to Consider

• Examine the child's environment, activities, and scheduling factors that may be discouraging rather than encouraging.

• Examine any personal liabilities on your part, such as being easy to anger, talking too much, being demanding, having to be in control, trying to be perfect, wanting to please.

• Assess your personal resources for building your encouragement skills. These are quali-ties or strengths such as a sense of humor, adeptness at problem solving, patience, or being perceptive.

Follow-Up

Your leader will provide time to discuss your results with the group at your next meeting. If your group does not meet again, plan a time to evaluate your efforts with others in your center who have taken the *TLC* class. If the results of the activity are unsatisfactory, decide how you can change your approach in the future.

Record Keeping (Optional)

You may find it helpful to log your observations and actions. The following format can be used for your log.

Daily Log   Child's Name: _____

	Situation	My Encouragement	Results
Monday			
Tuesday			
Wednesday			
Thursday			
Friday			

Points to Remember

1. From birth on, children form beliefs about their self-worth.

2. Encouragement helps children develop self-esteem.

3. Treat children with respect, and they will learn to treat others with respect.

4. Encouragement lets children decide for themselves if they are pleased with what they do. It doesn't demand perfection or make comparisons.

5. Praise and encouragement are *not* the same thing. Praise rewards a child and lets her feel accepted and valued only when she performs. Encouragement boosts a child and lets her accept and value herself.

6. Be concerned that your children *learn how to learn*, not that they perform perfectly.

7. Don't *push* children. Do *encourage* them by setting reasonable goals, accepting their efforts, and appreciating their improvements.

8. Guidelines for encouraging children to learn without using praise or pressure include:

   • Providing a developmentally appropriate environment which encourages learning experiences.

   • Following each child's interests.

   • De-emphasizing competition.

   • Asking open-ended questions.

   • Noticing all efforts, even small ones.

   • Making learning fun.

   • Helping children see the alternatives in challenging situations.

9. Teachers are role models for children. Both adults and children need to develop the courage to be imperfect.

10. Teachers who demonstrate strong self-esteem will help their children develop strong self-esteem and courage for facing life's challenges.

11. We all communicate with words and body language. Young children use body language long before they can speak. We see their feelings in their expressions and behavior.

12. We can use reflective listening to show understanding of the underlying meaning in a child's words. Like a mirror, we reflect what the child says.

13. Follow this formula to learn to use reflective listening: "You feel (<u>state the feeling</u>) because (<u>state the reason behind the feeling</u>)."

    • "You feel sorry because Mickey got hurt."

    • "You feel excited because it's snowing."

14. Children need to hear and learn words for their feelings.

15. Reflective listening is helpful when a child expresses emotions or when you believe the child has feelings that are not being expressed.

Just For You

Your Lifestyle Priorities

Starting in infancy, we all develop beliefs about who we are, who other people are, what is important in life, and how to belong. According to Alfred Adler, a pioneer in personality theory, the beliefs we develop and our ways of living out these beliefs form the basis of our lifestyle.*

Lifestyle is the characteristic pattern of our beliefs that influences our behavior throughout life. Here we are looking at lifestyle personality patterns as they apply to teachers. In Chapter 6, we will look at lifestyle in relation to working with parents.

Although each individual is unique, there are five lifestyle personality traits, or priorities, which often characterize how people interact with the world.

- *Control*—To feel in control of things

- *Perfectionism*—To do things right, to be perfect

- *Pleasing*—To please others

- *Being a Victim*—To feel that what happens is caused by others

- *Being a Martyr*—To feel overresponsible and overburdened, to feel that one is suffering

Most of us adopt one or two of these priorities as the way we characteristically deal with things.

You can find out which priorities you value most by a simple test. Priorities are related to what a person most wants to avoid. Which of the following situations would you *most want to avoid*? Put a 1 in front of it. Rank the others 2, 3, 4, and 5, with 2 being the situation you would next most want to avoid.

* To learn more about the personality priorities, read *The Effective Parent* by Don Dinkmeyer et al. (Circle Pines, MN: American Guidance Service, 1987); *The Basics of Understanding Your Lifestyle* by Don Dinkmeyer (Coral Springs, FL: CMTI Press, 1992); *Out of Apples* by Lee Schnebly (Tucson, AZ: Manzanas Press, 1984—write to Manzanas Press, 2641 N. Arcadia, Tucson, AZ 85712); *The Pleasers* by Kevin Leman (Old Tappan, N.J.: Fleming Revell, 1987); and *Kern Lifestyle Scale Interpretation Manual* by Roy Kern (Coral Springs, FL: CMTI Press, 1992). Or listen to the audiocassette *Lifestyle Interpretation* by Roy Kern (Coral Springs, FL: CMTI Press, 1982—write to CMTI Press, Box 8268, Coral Springs, FL 33065).

A. ___ Being embarrassed, having the unexpected occur, being out of control

B. ___ Being held responsible for your behavior and relationships

C. ___ Being rejected or disapproved of by others

D. ___ Being wrong, making mistakes

E. ___ Being overburdened and held responsible for the challenges of living

If you most want to avoid A, your major priority is most likely *Control*.

If you most want to avoid B, your priority is most likely being the *Victim*.

If you most want to avoid C, your priority is most likely *Pleasing*.

If you most want to avoid D, your priority is most likely *Perfectionism*.

If you most want to avoid E, your priority is most likely being a *Martyr*.

Now you can see how you value the five priorities.

Look at the Possible Lifestyle Priorities Chart on the next page. It lists some of the ways the different priorities can affect you, your teaching style, and the children you work with.

• How do your highest priorities affect your approach to teaching?

• How do your highest priorities affect your relationships with coworkers? Your personal relationships?

• How can your understanding of priorities help you become more effective in your relationships with children, coworkers, friends, and family?

Possible Lifestyle Priorities

	Control	Perfectionism	Pleasing	Victim	Martyr
Your Belief	I must be in control and get my way.	I control myself and others by being "perfect." I must always be at my best.	I must please others at all costs.	I am not responsible.	I am over-burdened. People expect too much.
Upside	Makes decisions, chooses and decides. Problem solver, organized.	Competent and capable. High standards, achievement oriented. Pays excess attention to detail, plans carefully. Strives to improve and avoid mistakes.	Others appreciate this person's concern. The person usually receives love and acceptance. Empathic, sensitive, tuned in to others, team player.	Tend to get service and sympathy from others because they pity them. Victims tend to display inadequacy and are often excused from functioning. Use discouragement to put others at their service.	People perceive the martyr as responsible.
Downside	Power oriented, challenges others. Not tuned to feelings. Tends to be self-centered.	The move to be perfect influences others to avoid being close. Not willing to risk mistakes. "Type A" personality. Sets impossible goals. Fears spontaneity. Overconcerned with being right.	Hard to say "no." Tends to evoke sympathy, pity. At times may be insistent on approval. Taken advantage of, lower self-esteem, tries to please others.	People tend to avoid the victim. Low self-esteem and reduced self-respect.	Continuously complains about suffering. Blames, believes it is always the other person's fault.
How Others React	Others tend to feel challenged and resistant. Want to resist being controlled.	Others feel they are not as much as they should be. They feel inferior, not meeting the standards.	Others feel positive at first, but later turned off by the continual demands for approval.	Other people tend to feel tired of hearing the victim's stories of how he/she has been used.	Others avoid the martyr because they are tired of the complaints.
Price You Pay	People tend to avoid and keep their distance.	Usually very responsible and totally involved. As a result, feels taken advantage of and over-burdened.	Less personal growth. Often feels not part of the group. Pleasers tend to put their needs second and feel less satisfied.	Has reduced self-esteem, courage. Lacks confidence.	Martyrs are excluded from the group. They are avoided because they have the same song all the time.
What You Want to Avoid	Avoids things being out of control, the unexpected, and being embarrassed.	Seeks to avoid meaninglessness and mistakes. Works on being perfect.	Rejection at all costs. It is important to get approval.	Wants to avoid being responsible for life and relationships.	Being held responsible for own behavior.

Adapted from: Don Dinkmeyer, Sr., *The Basics of Understanding Your Lifestyle* (Coral Springs, FL.: CMTI Press, 1991).

Chapter 3
Solving Problems with Young Children

What You Will Learn

- I-messages are a way to state your feelings without blaming.

- Children "own" some of their problems.

- Exploring alternatives is a five-step method to help solve problems owned either by children or teachers.

The way we communicate with children is an important part of teaching mutual respect. We want to share our feelings without being judgmental. This is especially important when we encounter problems with children. We need to address the problems and find solutions in ways that will not be discouraging. In this chapter we will look at respectful, encouraging ways to talk with children, prevent misbehavior, and solve problems with them.

Letting Children Know How You Feel: You-Messages and I-Messages

When we share our feelings and ideas with children, it's important to talk *with* them, not *at* them. This is especially true when dealing with children in a problem situation. There are two kinds of messages our words can give to children: you-messages and I-messages.

You-messages focus on the child, often in a fault-finding way.

- "You better stop that!"

- "You cry too much."

- "You really messed up this time."

- "You make me angry!"

You-messages put children down and are experienced by them as blaming, scolding, or nagging. You-messages usually contain the word *you*. They attack, insult, or pass judgment on a child. Adults often use you-messages in exasperation or to get quick results when children misbehave. But children who receive lots of you-messages are likely to begin feeling worthless, to fight back, or to stop listening. You-messages can discourage cooperation and contribute to low self-esteem.

I-messages focus on you, rather than your child. They don't label or blame. When you use an I-message, you simply tell how you feel.

A more effective, respectful way of communicating feelings is to use I-messages. I-messages describe how you feel when a child's behavior interferes with your rights or other children's rights. They focus on you, rather than on the child. I-messages don't label or blame. They simply tell how you feel.

To communicate your feelings in an I-message, follow these three steps:

1. State very specifically what behavior led to your feeling.

2. State what you are feeling.

3. Explain the consequences of the behavior for you.

The Three Parts of an I-Message

Like reflective listening, I-messages have a formula too. When learning to use I-messages, put your words together using these three parts:

1. *When* "When I see hitting . . .

2. *I feel* I feel worried . . .

3. *because* because somebody could get hurt."

- "When I see paint on the walls, I feel unhappy because it's hard to scrub off."

- "When I hear so much crying, I feel confused because I can't understand what you're trying to say to me."

I-messages help children focus on how their actions are received by others. By using I-messages, you show the importance of sharing feelings in a constructive way.

You help children learn to communicate their own feelings respectfully.

> *Pedro refuses to share his toys with Angela, another four-year-old. Their teacher responds with an I-message: "Pedro, when you won't let Angela play with any toys, I feel distracted, because the fighting keeps interrupting the story I'm reading to Tony and Isabel. And it looks like Angela feels hurt that you won't share any toys with her."*

This I-message may or may not solve the problem. But Pedro has received information about how his behavior affects four other people. Because he's been treated respectfully, Pedro's self-respect isn't damaged. He will likely be better able to focus on problem solving.

I-messages let us state our feelings calmly.

Avoid Angry I-Messages

It's important to keep hostile feelings out of your I-messages. Often, anger is the result of other feelings that you are not expressing. But if you speak in an angry or harsh way, it's very hard for children to believe they aren't being blamed for your anger.

> *One child might try to push another off the top of the climber, causing the second child to scream in alarm.*
>
> *On your way over, you might angrily shout, "Erin! Stop that . . . RIGHT NOW!" Then you might lecture Erin on how she and others could fall and get injured by fighting on the playground equipment.*

If you look at what led to the anger, you'll probably find fear—you were afraid Erin might get hurt. Once you are aware your fear can lead to anger, you might handle the situation in a different way. You could simply stop Erin's aggression by calling her name to distract her, getting her down, and then expressing your fear: "I get scared when people push on the climber. Someone could fall off and get hurt. It's important to take turns and play safely."

In dangerous situations like this, don't assume a child has learned the lesson about safety. Children need safety guidelines stated, restated, and reinforced many times. In situations like this, it is helpful to take the time to kneel or sit at the child's level. Make good eye contact while discussing what has happened and your concerns for the child's safety.

It will help to reassure the child, clearly communicate the lesson, and put you on the child's level for a personal pat or hug.

Of course, young children won't necessarily understand the problem from your point of view. Nevertheless, using I-messages shows that while you are upset about unacceptable behavior, you value and appreciate children enough to deal with the problem without yelling, blaming, or threatening. Children who constantly hear I-messages as a means of addressing problems are more likely, as they grow older, to appreciate the rights and feelings of others.

Send Friendly I-Messages Too!

Friendly I-messages are effective ways to give children positive attention and encouragement:

- "I feel happy when I see children putting things away because it means we'll find what we need next time."

- "I really like your smile."

- "I enjoyed our story time today! Everybody was cooperating and listening to the story."

- "I like to hear you jabbering—I can tell you're a happy baby today."

Keep Your Expectations Realistic

I-messages are a way of communicating and guiding—not a way to control. Children may or may not stop unpleasant behavior because they've been understood or because they understand us.

Like reflective listening, I-messages improve communication. They can influence behavior in a particular situation. They won't guarantee better behavior, but they will tell a child he is important enough to be heard and spoken to with respect.

Begin Using I-Messages Early

I-messages can be used with even the youngest children. Babies will miss the meaning of the words. But they will not miss the sharing attitude of mutual respect shown in your voice and face.

- "I see you really like that rattle! I'm glad to see you so happy!"

- "When you lie still like this, diaper changing goes fast. Then we both feel happy!"

The younger the child, the simpler the I-message must be:

- "I get scared when you climb up on the counter. You could fall off and get hurt."

- "I don't like the screaming. It hurts my ears."

Toddlers and preschoolers understand both the attitude and the meaning of the words:

- "I see you're sharing the sand table with Tyler. I'm happy you can dig together."

- "I'm glad you're helping Wendy zip her jacket. It's nice to be able to help a friend."

Young children won't necessarily understand the problem from your point of view.

71

I-messages establish an atmosphere of mutual respect with all young children. They also help preschoolers and kindergartners grow less self-centered and begin to understand and respect the feelings of others.

Children who constantly hear I-messages as a means of addressing problems are more likely, as they grow older, to appreciate the rights and feelings of others.

Solving Problems with Children

When problems arise concerning children's behavior, we can ask ourselves, "Who does this problem belong to? Me? Or the child? In other words, who 'owns' the problem?"[1]

Who Owns the Problem?

Some problems are teacher-owned problems because children don't have the ability to solve them at this point in their development. Other problems belong to the children themselves. In these cases, our job as teachers is to help them learn how to take responsibility for their problems and find ways of solving them. The first step in solving a problem is deciding who owns it.

The person who owns a problem is the one who is responsible for handling it. It's easy to feel we own all children's problems. But when teachers try to solve all problems, children don't get the chance to learn how to be responsible for themselves. It isn't possible or desirable for any teacher to be "Super Problem Solver"! Recognizing *who* owns the problem in a given situation helps you decide what, if any, action to take in that situation.

Who Owns the Problem?

How do teachers determine which problems belong to them and which belong to the children? To decide who owns a problem, ask yourself four questions:

1. Does the problem interfere with my rights as a person?

2. Does it involve the safety of the child or others?

3. Does it involve the protection of property?

4. Is the child developmentally *in*capable of owning or solving this problem?

If the answer to *any one* of these questions is yes, then you own the problem.

If the answer to *all* of these questions is no, then the child may own the problem—depending on the child's age and what the problem is.

In the case of infants and toddlers, teachers will own most of the problems. But the rightful ownership of many problems can be transferred to children as they grow older.

If six-month-old Kim is crying because she's hungry, it's the teacher's problem. At six months, Kim can't feed herself. On the other hand, if four-year-old Robert doesn't eat lunch because it looks "yucky" and then gets hungry before snack-time, it's Robert's problem. He is old enough to understand the natural consequences of not eating at mealtimes.

If ten-month-old Jasmai is fussing because she has a dirty diaper and is uncomfortable, it's her teacher's problem. On the other hand, if five-year-old Amy is complaining because she spilled water on her dress and doesn't like the feel of wet clothes, it's Amy's problem. At five, Amy is old enough to understand that while accidents do happen, she did the spilling—it's not anyone else's responsibility.

Examples of Teacher-Owned Problems

Two-year-old Daryl starts to color on the walls.

Two-year-old Todd grabs Carey's blanket. Carey bites him.

Three-year-old Yolanda is dawdling while the rest of the children are getting dressed to go play in the snow. Finally, the rest of the group is all dressed for outdoors. Yolanda still doesn't have her snowsuit or boots on, and the rest of the group is getting impatient and restless.

Examples of Child-Owned Problems

Four-year-old Steven complains the other children won't let him play. You notice he gets aggressive and takes toys from others.

You could say, "You feel sad because the others won't let you play." Then you might say, "I notice sometimes you try to take a toy from the others. Maybe they don't like that. Then they don't want to play with you." Then you could ask Steven for ideas on how he could play so others would want him there. If he has trouble thinking of ideas, make a suggestion. Finally, you may have to take Steven to the group and tell the children he's decided to play nicely.

> *Four-year-old Kate sits at the snack table sobbing. When the teacher asks her what's wrong, Kate says, "Janie won't sit next to me."*

Kate may need to be reminded she can't make other people do things, but she can make a different choice for herself in the situation—such as choosing someone else to sit by.

> *Two-year-old Eli stands by the climber yelling. His legs aren't long enough to reach the first rung in order to climb up.*

You can listen and sympathize with Eli's feelings, but there's nothing you can do about his legs! You can help him find a place to climb that's safe for small children.

Sometimes you'll want to let the child cope on his own. At other times, you will help the child find a solution.

The younger children are, the more they depend on us for care. But what they can do on their own, they need to be allowed to do. Being allowed to solve their own problems builds self-confidence in children.

> *Six-month-old Eugenia wants a rattle that lies just beyond her reach. She struggles to reach it. The teacher is tempted to get it for her, but holds back, giving Eugenia a chance to retrieve the rattle herself. The teacher encourages Eugenia by saying, "You can do it. You're almost there." Eugenia feels the gentle support in the teacher's words. When she finally reaches the rattle, her teacher says, "You got it! Good for you, Eugenia!"*

Cooperating to Solve Problems

Deciding who owns a problem gives you a clue to action. When you own the problem, you are the one who needs to do something about it. When the child owns the problem, your action will depend on the nature of the problem and the developmental stage of the child. Sometimes you'll want the child to cope on his own. At other times, you will help the child find a solution.

Whenever you or a child owns a problem, you can do one or more of the following:

- Allow the child to find a solution on his own, without adult intervention.

- Use reflective listening or an I-message.

- Make sure the child knows the consequences of his behavior.

- Explore alternatives with the child.

Exploring Alternatives

Earlier in this chapter, we discussed how reflective listening and I-messages can help solve or lessen behavior problems. But they may not always be enough to solve the problems.

Teachers can also use a method called exploring alternatives. *Exploring alternatives is a five-step process of helping children look at different ways to solve a problem.* The method applies to both teacher-owned and child-owned problems.[2]

The Five Steps of Exploring Alternatives

1. **Understand the problem.** Make sure the problem is clear to both you and the child. Use reflective listening and I-messages to show your understanding of the child's feelings and to express your own.

2. **Use brainstorming to find possible solutions or alternatives.** Ask the child for suggestions, or guide him by offering tentative suggestions ("What might happen if you . . . ?"). Offer suggestions yourself if the child is having difficulty. At this step, don't judge or evaluate any suggested solutions. Just talk about possibilities.

3. **Consider the suggested solutions.** What does the child think of each possible solution? What do you think?

4. **Choose a solution.** Cooperate with the child to find a solution acceptable to both of you.

5. **Get a commitment to a solution and set a time to evaluate it.** Decide together how long to use the solution. Set a specific time to talk about how well each person thinks the solution is working.

With very young children, you will want to explore alternatives as simply and briefly as possible. For example, in brainstorming, you may guide the child to only two or three solutions. You may even accept a single suggestion, if it seems workable.

Three-year-old Evan has built a tower out of Legos. Now it's time to clean up, but Evan doesn't want to take his tower apart. His teacher, Mr. Calhoun, explains that the class needs the table for snacktime. Mr. Calhoun says, "Evan, we can't eat our snack with Legos all over the table." Evan tells the teacher he wants to show the tower to his dad when he comes to pick him up. Evan and Mr. Calhoun agree to carefully move the tower to the countertop and save it until the end of the day. Then Evan cheerfully picks up the rest of the Legos, so the table can be used for snacktime.

Often, too, situations can be handled by giving a child a simple choice. For example, two children are about to come to blows over a toy. You could say, "Can you two solve this problem fairly, or do you need to stop playing together for awhile?"

Preschoolers can take more responsibility for finding solutions to their own problems.

Two four-year-olds—Michael and Ramon—come complaining to you, their teacher:

Michael: *He took my blocks!*
Ramon: *I had them first!*
Michael: *No you didn't, I had them first!*
You: *Boys, you have a problem. Both of you seem angry with the other about the blocks. How can you solve your problem?*

You use the word "your" to make it clear the problem is theirs to solve. Both boys try to continue the argument about who had the blocks first.

You: *Boys, I can't help you with this problem if you keep arguing. How can you solve your problem?*
Michael: *He can use them after I get through.*
Ramon: *No, I want them first!*
You: *You both want them first! How can that work? Can you think of another idea?*
Ramon: *Maybe we could build something together.*
Michael: *I don't wanna do it together.*
Ramon: *We could build a racetrack.*
Michael: *No, I wanna build a spaceship.*
Ramon: *Yeah! A spaceship. Let's do that.*
Michael: *Okay.*
You: *Well it looks like you boys worked it out—you thought of a way to share the blocks. Let's talk about it right before lunch and see how your idea worked.*

If the boys hadn't agreed, you as teacher might have suggested dividing the blocks or putting them away for awhile.

Dealing with Problems the Teacher Owns

The goal of problem solving is to find an effective solution that's respectful to both you *and* the child. Children are more likely to cooperate when they feel that they have some power and choice in a situation and that their feelings and wishes are valued.

Which action you choose in dealing with teacher-owned problems depends on the child's age, the type of problem, and how often the problem happens.

When you pick up sixteen-month-old Mindy, she knocks your glasses off. You put them back on and say, "When my glasses are knocked off, I'm afraid they will break." A few minutes later, Mindy knocks the glasses off again. You gently place Mindy on the floor and tell her, "I can't let you grab my glasses, so I'm putting you down." Later when Mindy wants to be picked up again, you can give her another chance. "Do you want to sit on my lap again? Okay. But if you grab my glasses, I will put you down."

Here you used an I-message, stated consequences, and followed through. Mindy hasn't had much practice at controlling her behavior, so she will probably grab the glasses again. Knowing what will happen helps her learn control. Whenever Mindy grabs, she gets put down. She begins to learn the consequence of her action.

Our goal is to increase our children's sense of responsibility for solving their own problems.

Two-year-old Fumiko is upset because there is a substitute teacher. She keeps testing the limits and doesn't want to lie down on her cot at naptime. The substitute acknowledges Fumiko's feelings by saying, "I know you wish your teacher were here. She's sick today. I can tell you miss her, but you still need to lie down on your cot. You lie down now, and I'll rub your back to help you relax."

Treating children with mutual respect and allowing them some power and choice in a situation is important for problem solving with preschoolers, too.

Five-year-old Tom keeps interrupting stories at circle time with attempts to be funny. Tom feels a sense of power in capturing the group and the teacher's attention. The teacher decides to discuss his behavior with him just prior to today's storytime.

Step 1   *(Understand the problem)*

Teacher: *Tom, I want to talk with you because storytime is coming up soon. When you interrupt me while I'm reading a story, I feel worried that the other children can't hear the story. How do you feel?*

Tom: *I don't know. I just like to talk because it's funny.*

Teacher: *So, you really enjoy making people laugh.*

Tom: *Yeah!*

Step 2   *(Use brainstorming to find possible solutions or alternatives)*

Teacher: *Okay. You want to be funny and the other children want to hear a story. How can we solve this problem?*

Tom: *Maybe I could tell them a funny story!*

Teacher: *Okay, that's one idea. Do you have any other ideas?*

Tom: *Nope!*

Step 3   *(Consider the suggested solutions) and*

Step 4   *(Choose a solution)*

Teacher: *All right. I'm willing to go along with that as long as it's just one story each time, and you are quiet the rest of the time so I can read a story to everybody. Okay?*

Tom: *Okay.*

The teacher asks Tom if he wants to tell his story at the beginning or at the end of storytime. Tom chooses the beginning of the period.

> **Step 5** *(Get a commitment to a solution and set a time to evaluate it)*
>
> **Teacher:** *Okay, let's write it out to show we're both willing to work together. Shall we try our agreement at storytime and talk about it afterwards to see how our agreement worked?*
>
> **Tom:** *Yeah.*
>
> *The teacher writes out the agreement and signs it. Tom can write his name, so he signs it too.*
>
> ### Sample Agreement
>
> 1. Tom gets to tell one funny story at the beginning of storytime.
>
> 2. Tom agrees to not interrupt the group after he tells his story.
>
> _____   _____
> *(Teacher's signature)*   *(Child's signature or mark)*

If the plan is successful, the teacher and Tom can continue the agreement. Some of the other children may want to join in too. A "funny story" time could be established that would be a form of self-expression.

If the plan is unsuccessful, the teacher and Tom may have to discuss a different arrangement. For example, if Tom persists in interrupting, the teacher may have to ask him to be apart from the group during storytime until he's ready to listen.

Helping Children Solve Problems

Exploring alternatives is also useful in helping children settle arguments. It is a way of giving ownership of children's quarrels to the children.

> *In the three-year-old-room, Camilla and Diana both want to use the wagon to give their dolls a ride. They start pushing and shoving each other. Their teacher comes over and says, "It looks like you both want the wagon. How can we solve this problem?"*
>
> *Camilla says, "We can take turns, but I get it first." Diana says, "You could pull me and my doll." The teacher says encouragingly, "Those both sound like good ideas. Which one do you want to try?"*
>
> *Camilla offers, "I'll pull and you ride. Then you can pull me and my doll."*

Sometimes conflicts may involve groups of children.

> *Three five-year-olds are playing in the housekeeping area, setting the table with dishes and feeding the dolls with spoons and cups. Another group of children wants to have a pretend picnic in the block area, so they run into the housekeeping area and grab the dishes from the table. The first group runs to the teacher to complain.*
>
> *The teacher, Mr. Grant, comes over to establish peace. He asks each group what the problem is. The first group says, "We need the dishes to play house. We had them first, and those guys came and grabbed them." The second group says, "We need dishes for our picnic. They already had a turn with the dishes! They should have to share!"*
>
> *Mr. Grant suggests that the children try to come up with their own solution. One child says, "Well, maybe they can use the dishes for their picnic after we say we're done with them." Another child says, "Why don't they look in the cabinet and see if there are more dishes we aren't using?" A child from the picnic group decides to investigate and finds there are indeed dishes that aren't being used.*
>
> *The picnic group gets some extra dishes out of the cabinet and goes off to set them out on a blanket. After more discussion among themselves, they come back to the house area and invite the other children to bring their dolls to the picnic.*

Exploring alternatives can't always produce results that satisfy everyone's desires in a conflict situation. But as a method of problem solving, it's a process worth introducing to children early in their development.

Problem Solving with Very Young Children

Eleanor Reynolds—author of *Guiding Young Children*—teaches young children to solve relationship problems beginning when infants are first able to move around.[3] As infants begin to travel, they will inevitably bump into each other and grab one another's toys.

Reynolds notes that when negotiating with infants or preverbal toddlers, the teacher plays a special role. It's her job to put herself in the place of each child, to guess what the problem really is, and to express it verbally for each child. Unless the children are clearly showing a preference for a solution, the teacher can provide them ideas from which to choose. The tendency may be for teachers to provide ideas too quickly, without waiting for cues from the children. It's important to wait, giving preverbal children time to indicate their wishes.

A preverbal child is not yet able to communicate through words.

One-year-old Sarah takes a stuffed animal from ten-month-old Billy. Billy starts to cry. The teacher, Ms. Taylor, begins by reflecting Billy's feelings. "You're sad because Sarah took your bear." She then directs her attention to Sarah. "Sarah, Billy's sad because you took his bear."

Billy begins to cry louder. Ms. Taylor says to Sarah, "It sounds like Billy's really mad now—he's telling you to give it back." Sarah looks at her with a blank look on her face and shakes the bear up and down. "You really like the bear," Ms. Taylor says, "but Billy wants it back." Sarah turns away, continuing to bang the bear on the floor. Ms. Taylor turns to Billy, who's continuing to cry. "It looks like Sarah wants to keep the bear," she says. Billy looks at the bear and cries harder.

Ms. Taylor leaves for a moment and locates two more stuffed animals. She brings them to the children and places the animals between them. "Sarah, would you like to play with the tiger or the dog?" Sarah looks at the animals and picks up the tiger. "I see you like the tiger." Ms. Taylor gives the bear back to Billy and says to both children, "It looks like the problem is solved because now you both have an animal to play with."

While the children would not understand the words, they get the message from their teacher's concern and tone of voice. If Sarah had insisted on keeping the bear, Ms. Taylor could offer Billy the other animals. If he would not accept them, she might take the bear from Sarah, saying, "Billy really wants the bear back. You can pick one of the other animals." If Sarah complained, Ms. Taylor could reflect her feelings.

When a child gets physically aggressive with another child, Reynolds teaches the victim how to say "stop." She shows children how to put up a hand as a gesture to the other person to quit. With infants, she holds up their hands for them. Verbal children are also taught to say the word "stop."

Problem Solving with Older Children

Children gain new problem-solving abilities when they learn to talk. As with other skills, children develop in this area at their own rates. Some children will be ready for verbal problem solving as older toddlers. Others may develop this skill later. Teachers want to be sensitive to the level of each child's readiness to learn and practice problem-solving skills.

Be patient in encouraging children to use their words.

Children who come to you complaining about their treatment from others can be told to tell the other child how they feel and what they want.

- "I don't like it when you push me."

- "Stop calling me boo-boo head. My name is _____."

- "It hurts when you hit me. Be gentle."

You can stand nearby and observe the interaction. If the children seem to be handling the situation, don't interfere. Children need to learn how to handle problems on their own. Initially you may have to coach them on following the steps of negotiation:

- "Tell George what happened and how you feel . . . George, please listen to what Julie is telling you."

If, however, the interchange begins to get physical, you can intervene and help them negotiate.

Clare Cherry—author of *Please Don't Sit on the Kids*—points out that children from three to five years old can learn to conduct problem-solving discussions with varying degrees of skill.[4]

Four-year-old Omar comes to his teacher complaining that Sylvia won't give him the airplane even though he asked for it. The teacher points out that Sylvia had the airplane first, but Omar still isn't satisfied. The teacher decides to problem solve with both children.

Step 1	*(Understand the problem)*
Teacher:	*Omar, tell me what the problem is.*
Omar:	*I want the airplane, and Sylvia won't give it to me.*
Teacher:	*Sylvia?*
Sylvia:	*I had it first, and he tried to grab it.*
Step 2	*(Use brainstorming to find possible solutions or alternatives)*
Teacher:	*Let's think of some ways to solve this together.*

Possibilities might include taking turns, Omar choosing to play with something else, or Omar joining the airplane play while waiting for a turn with the plane by building a runway with blocks.

Step 3	*(Consider the suggested solutions)*
Teacher:	*Omar, you can't grab the plane from Sylvia. Which idea do you both want to use to solve this problem?*
Step 4	*(Choose a solution)*

Omar:	*I think I'll build a runway. Then I can use it when I take my turn with the plane.*
Sylvia:	*Yeah. Let's take turns.*
Step 5	*(Get a commitment to a solution and set a time to evaluate it)*
Teacher:	*That sounds like a good solution. I'll come over later to see what the airport looks like.*

Three-year-olds will need more involvement from you, but older fours and fives can eventually learn to handle most discussions on their own.

Cherry suggests that teachers train children in the rules of discussion. She teaches children to:

- Listen to, and look at, each child who is speaking. You don't have to agree with a person's feelings, just listen.

- State what you think happened and how you feel. If the child you're talking to is not listening, tell him directly that you are talking to him, and you would like him to listen.

- Together, decide what you will do if something like this happens again.[5]

The Talk-It-Over Place

Some teachers establish a place where children can talk over their disputes.[6] The area can be called the Talk-It-Over-Place. It should be a special area used only for that purpose. There can be chairs or a rug for the children to sit on. The goal is to increase the children's sense of responsibility for solving their own problems. The process works like this:

- Children who bring a dispute to you, or who quarrel to the point where you must intervene, are asked to go to the Talk-It-Over Place.

- Instruct the children to talk over their problem and come to a decision. Tell them they can return to play when they are ready to play together cooperatively.

- Some children will not discuss the issue and may end up laughing or sitting quietly. That's okay—the major point is that they have stopped the conflict.

- If the conflict continues after they return to play, tell the children they need more time to talk it over, and you will check with them in a few minutes.

- If they still aren't ready, tell them they will have to be involved in separate activities for awhile.

The Talk-It-Over Place is very effective in settling disputes. After using this technique for awhile, you will find that children who bicker will know they will be asked to go to the Talk-It-Over Place when you approach them about their behavior. Some children will automatically go to the Talk-It-Over-Place when they have a dispute.

Introduce this concept to the children individually or in a group. That way, they will know what to expect.

Group Meeting for Problem Solving and Decision Making*

Preschoolers can learn to solve problems together and practice democratic decision making through large and small group meetings. There are three types of group meetings: rule-making, planning, and problem-solving.

---

* Many of the ideas in this section were contributed by Kathy Walton, Director of the Adlerian Child Care Centers, Columbia, South Carolina and Yolanda Uribe, former Coordinator of Bilingual Early Childhood Education for Sunnyside School District, Tucson, Arizona.

Rule-Making Meetings

The teacher helps the children understand the rules. In some situations, the children can help develop the rules. When children help make the rules, they are more likely to follow them. Here are some examples of rules children can help establish:

- Routines. "Do we want storytime before snacktime or after?" "Should we wait for everyone to be ready to go outside, or go outside one at a time?"

- Care of equipment. "Where should we put the puzzle pieces?" (In the same tub or in any tub that's handy?) "What happens if we put them in different tubs? In the same tub?"

- Deciding where items go on shelves and how they get handled. For example, do the children want the teacher to hand out crayons, or do they want to freely choose their own?

Planning Meetings

Teachers and children can use group meetings to plan activities. Making plans and carrying them out is part of an effective learning experience. Some situations call for fairly simple planning. Even toddlers may be able to follow the teacher's lead at a simple level:

- "Tomorrow is Miss Shankar's last day because she's moving far away. How can we tell her we'll miss her? What can we do so she'll remember us?"

Other situations may call for more complicated planning. Preschoolers can handle this kind of thinking.

> *One day the group is going to plant some seeds. The planning discussion focuses on what items the children think they will need to accomplish the task. One child says a towel is needed in case water is spilled. The teacher writes out the plans and illustrates the children's decisions.*

Of course there will be times when the best plans fail to foresee everything. The teacher can use these situations to ask the children to do some on-the-spot problem solving.

Working with Parents
In a note, you may want to let parents know you are working with the children on finding solutions and alternatives in problem situations. Share the five steps of exploring alternatives with them. Emphasize that it's important to the children's development to ask them to think cooperatively about solutions to problems.

> *Perhaps a child pours too much water into a planting pot. The towel won't solve this problem. The teacher could say, "Now what can we do?" Another child might suggest using a container for pouring out the excess water.*

In a follow-up discussion with preschoolers, it's helpful to ask the children how they think the plans worked out. Write down what the children say. Children have great interest in having their own experiences written down. Writing out plans, instructions, and experiences has an additional benefit—it encourages interest in the written word.

Problem-Solving Meetings

The teacher presents a problem to the children and asks for their help in solving it. Depending on their age and developmental level, children may participate in group decisions to varying degrees. Begin involving three-year-olds in making choices in small groups of two or three children.

- "There's only room for two children in the spaceship and three children want to play. What should we do?"

- "When we eat lunch together, some children eat faster than others. What might they do while they're waiting for the rest of our group to finish?"

Older threes and fours can start making simple choices based on past experience:

As the teacher, you might use circle time to discuss with the four-year-olds whether they are ready to go outside on their own instead of waiting for the whole group. Through a show of hands, the children decide they want to try it on their own. Immediately after the outside time, you and the group evaluate what happened.

As children gain experience in making simple choices and experience consequences, they become ready to make independent suggestions in planning meetings. This generally occurs with fours and fives. When there is a problem that involves all or most of the group, it can be discussed in a group problem-solving meeting.

In Mrs. Johns' group of five-year-olds, the children have not been using the climber safely. Mrs. Johns tells the children she will have to close the climber unless they have some ideas on how to use it safely. This way, the children realize the situation is their problem. If they want to use the climber, they will need to make suggestions and stick to them.

Procedures for Problem-Solving Meetings

1. **Introduce the problem through a story, role play, or puppets.***

2. **Personalize the problem.** "Has anything like this ever happened to you?"

3. **Discuss children's feelings.**

4. **Ask for suggestions to solve the problem.** "What could you do to help?"

With very young children, you will want to explore alternatives as simply and briefly as possible.

Recently, there has been a rash of name-calling incidents involving a number of children. You introduce the problem by telling or reading a story that illustrates the same problem. Then you ask the children about the name calling over the past few days. The goal of such a discussion is to help the children understand the problem, empathize, and reach a solution.

Another way to handle a problem-solving meeting is to simply address the problem directly:

---

*Two good sources of stories, role plays, and puppets are: Don Dinkmeyer Sr. and Don Dinkmeyer Jr., *Developing Understanding of Self and Others (DUSO) 1 Revised* (Circle Pines, MN: American Guidance Service, 1982), and Duane E. Davis, *My Friends & Me* (Circle Pines, MN: American Guidance Service, 1988). These activities not only help the group understand concepts, but help develop cooperative problem solving.

> *A teacher is concerned because four-year-olds are making fun of one girl who wears a hearing aid. After asking the children to stop, the teacher decides to call a group meeting to discuss the issue.*
>
> **Teacher:** *I want to talk to you about a problem we're having. It hurts Molly's feelings when she gets teased about wearing a hearing aid. Her hearing aid is a tool to help her hear better, just like my glasses are a tool to help me see better.*
>
> **Heather:** *Why does Molly wear the hearing aid? It looks funny.*
>
> **Teacher:** *The hearing aid makes sounds louder for Molly, so she can hear you better when you talk.*
>
> **Chris:** *I'm scared I might catch her earsickness if I get near to her.*
>
> **Alonzo:** *Why doesn't somebody fix her ears?*
>
> **Teacher:** *Molly isn't sick. Nobody can catch ear problems from her, but nobody can fix her ears, either. Molly was born hearing less than you or me. The hearing aid is an important tool to help her. She needs it, and she needs for you to understand why she wears it.*

In problem-solving meetings children get important practice in thinking cooperatively together.

In Mrs. Pozzini's kindergarten, children keep losing notes and permission slips that are supposed to be delivered to their parents. The teacher calls a group meeting.

Teacher: *Your parents and I are having a problem. I want them to get the letters and permission slips I'm sending home to them. Your parents need to know that you'll deliver the messages to them.*

Justin: *My backpack has a hole. Notes keep falling out.*

Vicki: *I put the notes in my jacket pocket, but then I forget to take them out.*

Andy: *I leave my notes on the bus.*

Teacher: *It sounds like there are a lot of different reasons why messages don't make it home.*

The teacher asks the children for suggestions to solve the problem. They think it over and come up with several suggestions, including the one the group decides to try—large manila envelopes with the children's names on them. The group decides to use the envelopes each day to take notes to and from home.

A week later, the solution is evaluated by the whole group and found to be very successful. Everyone is pleased—children, teachers, and parents.

You and Your Relationships

The question "Who owns the problem?" can be useful to consider in family, personal, and work situations. As teachers, we often feel responsible for other people's well-being. But our sense of responsibility can lead to guilty feelings if we attempt to solve every problem that comes along. Healthy relationships call for *mutual* problem solving. When problems arise, first ask, "Who owns this problem?" The answer will provide the starting place for finding a solution.

Not all problems are solved so easily. Also, some of the children may not follow through on putting the solutions into practice. You may have to remind them of their decisions.

As teachers, we hope a problem-solving meeting will end with a solution. But this is not always the case. Sometimes the children won't come up with a way to solve the problem in the discussion, but you may notice children being more aware of their behavior after the discussion.

Problem-solving skills contribute to children's self-esteem. They give children the ability to be actively engaged in life. Children who learn early to take responsibility for tackling their own problems are developing skills that will help them become self-reliant, confident people as they mature.

Notes

1. Thomas Gordon, *Teacher Effectiveness Training* (New York: David McKay, 1974), pp. 38-40.

2. Don Dinkmeyer, Gary D. McKay, and James S. Dinkmeyer, *Parenting Young Children* (Circle Pines, MN: American Guidance Service, 1989), p. 90.

3. Eleanor Reynolds, *Guiding Young Children: A Child Centered Approach* (Mountain View, CA: Mayfield, 1990), pp. 113-152.

4. Clare Cherry, *Please Don't Sit on the Kids: Alternatives to Punitive Discipline* (Belmont, CA: David S. Lake, 1983), pp. 152, 155.

5. Cherry, pp. 151-152.

6. Grace Mitchell, *A Very Practical Guide to Discipline with Young Children* (Marshfield, MA: Telshare, 1982), pp. 143-144.

Problem Situations

Infant. Thirteen-month-old Mellie is the youngest of five children in a child care home. The other children are between the ages of two and five years old. At the end of the day Mrs. Robb, the child care provider, takes all the children out to play in a fenced play area. This week the children have been playing a kick-and-catch game with a volleyball. Mellie wants to join in, but the back-and-forth play is too fast for her. Mellie cries and often falls as she tries to run in and out among the others after the ball.

1. Who owns the problem of Mellie's crying and falling?

2. What are some ways Mrs. Robb might help Mellie in this situation?

Toddler. June and Mike, both two-and-a-half, are playing together in the sandbox. June is systematically throwing sand down Mike's shirt and Mike is hitting June in the chest and crying, "Quit it!"

1. Who owns this problem?

2. How can the children's teacher help them explore alternatives to solve the problem?

Preschooler. Five-year-old Jill has just come to her teacher, Mr. James, and told him that Calvin, another five-year-old, is smearing black paint over a mural the children are painting together. Mr. James looks and sees that two children are trying to push Calvin away. Calvin has indeed smeared streaks of black paint over the children's artwork.

1. Who owns this problem?

2. How can the children's teacher work with the children to solve the problem?

Reflective Listening and I-Messages

Use reflective listening and I-messages to help children feel respected. Over time, communicating in these ways can help them understand what they feel and how others feel.

Age Range	Reflective Listening	I-Messages
Infants Use feeling vocabulary with infants. Respond to their nonverbal messages, and let them begin to learn how they are feeling. Though babies won't understand many of your words, they will sense your feelings.	"You can't reach the ball—you feel angry." "You're scared with so many children here." "You're very happy to have your bear."	"When you feel sick, I feel sad." "When I see you smiling, I feel happy too!" "I wish I knew why you're crying."
Toddlers Since toddlers are becoming verbal, respond more to their words. Yet still watch their behavior to pick up their feelings.	"You sound pretty angry because I won't let you hit Susie." "You're really excited to get to play with Jimmy." "Your face says you're sad—do you think this is unfair?"	"When I don't know why you're crying, I don't know how to help." "When you say you hate me, I feel sad, but I still like you." "When you throw toys, I worry that someone might get hurt."
Preschoolers Preschoolers' ability to reason is better developed. Respond more to verbal messages, but still look for nonverbal ones. Use more specific responses to their feelings than the general mad, upset, angry, sad, and glad. You can guess how preschoolers feel—they will usually redirect you if you're wrong.	"You look disappointed with your drawing." "Is it possible that you're feeling left out?" "You feel excited because we're going to the zoo."	"When you jump on the teeter totter, I get scared because you might get hurt." "I feel disappointed when people don't listen to each other because it seems like we don't care about what others have to say." "I feel good when everyone is playing nicely. It shows you're learning to get along with others."

Who Owns the Problems?

To determine problem ownership, ask yourself: "Does this problem interfere with my rights as a person? Does it involve the safety of the child or others? Does it involve the protection of property? Is the child developmentally incapable of 'owning' or solving the problem?" If the answer to any *one* of these questions is *yes*, then you own the problem. If the answer to *each* of the questions if *no,* then the child may own the problem—depending on the child's age.

	Situation	Who Owns Problem?	Appropriate Response
Infants	The younger the child, the more likely it is that the teacher will own the problem. With an infant, more safety and developmental concerns take precedence. If a six-month-old is crying because he is hungry or wet, you own the problem because it involves the safety (health) of the child.		
Toddlers	Eighteen-month-old wants more cookies than allowed, so toddler throws a tantrum.	Child	First, use reflective listening: "I see you are really angry that you're not getting more cookies." Then, explore alternatives: "You may have some cut-up fruit." Third, ignore the tantrum if child persists.
	Toddler refuses to be buckled into van seat on field trip.	Teacher	Child must be buckled in for safety: "You don't like the seat belt, but to be safe, you must be buckled in."
	Toddler chooses not to wear jacket on cold day.	Child	Toddler will go outside and come back in when cold: "I see you got cold. Would you like to put a jacket on so you won't be as cold when you go back outside?"
Preschoolers	Two three-year-olds fight over toy.	Child	"I see you both want to play with the toy. Can you think of a way to share it?" If they don't cooperate, separate them. If there is no hitting, let them work it out on their own.
	Four-year-old spills his juice.	Child	Give him the opportunity to clean up spill.
	Five-year-old refuses to take prescribed medication.	Teacher	Child needs to take medication. "It is very important that you take this medication. Then you will feel better." If child still refuses, discuss with parent.

Applying Your Skills

Practice identifying "who owns the problem." Once ownership of the problem is identified, decide what you can do based on the skills you have learned thus far in *TLC*. You may decide to begin with just one or two children.

Things to Consider

• Examine the child's environment, activities, and scheduling factors which may be contributing to the problem.

• Examine any personal liabilities on your part, such as being easy to anger, talking too much, being demanding, having to be in control, trying to be perfect, wanting to please.

• Assess your personal resources for solving this problem. These are qualities or strengths such as a sense of humor, skill at problem solving, patience, or being perceptive.

Follow-Up

Your leader will provide time to discuss your results with the group at your next meeting. If your group does not meet again, plan a time to evaluate your efforts with others in your center who have taken the *TLC* class. If the results of the assignment are unsatisfactory, decide how you can change your approach in the future.

Record Keeping (Optional)

You may find it helpful to log your observations and actions. The following format can be used for your log.

Daily Log   Child's Name: _____

	Problem	Who Owns?	My Action	Results
Monday				
Tuesday				
Wednesday				
Thursday				
Friday				

Points to Remember

1. When talking with children, avoid using you-messages, which can blame or put them down. Instead, use I-messages, which tell how you feel and don't blame or nag.

2. Follow this formula to learn to use "I-messages":

   When   "When I see hitting . . .

   I feel   I feel worried . . .

   because   because somebody could get hurt."

3. I-messages are ways to communicate with and influence children. They are not methods of control or guarantees of better behavior.

4. The person who owns a problem is the one responsible for handling it. Sometimes that's the teacher, sometimes the child.

5. To decide who owns a problem, ask yourself four questions:

   • Does the problem interfere with my rights as a person?

   • Does it involve the safety of the child or other children?

   • Does it involve protection of property?

   • Is the child developmentally *in*capable of "owning" or solving the problem at this stage of his growth?

   Any one *yes* answer means it's a teacher-owned problem.

   Four *no* answers means it's a child-owned problem.

6. Whether you or the children own a problem, there are various possible actions you can take to find a solution:

   • Allow the child to find a solution independently.

   • Use reflective listening or I-messages.

   • Make sure the child knows the consequence of her behavior.

   • Explore alternatives with the child.

7. Exploring alternatives is a five-step method of finding solutions:

   • Understand the problem.

   • Use brainstorming to find possible solutions or alternatives.

   • Consider the suggested solutions.

   • Choose a solution.

   • Get a commitment to a solution and set a time to evaluate it.

8. Exploring alternatives can be used when:

   • the teacher has a problem with one or more children.

   • an individual child has a problem.

   • two or more children have a problem getting along.

   • making plans and decisions in center meetings.

9. Group meetings help preschoolers and kindergartners:

   • participate in making rules.

   • plan learning activities.

   • solve problems involving the entire group.

Handing Conflict in Adult Relationships

Exploring alternatives can be used to address problems with children. It can also be used when a conflict occurs with a co-worker, spouse, friend, or relative. You can use the steps of exploring alternatives to negotiate agreements:*

1. Understand the problem.

2. Use brainstorming to find possible solutions or alternatives.

3. Consider the suggested solutions.

4. Choose a solution.

5. Get a commitment to a solution and set a time to evaluate it.

   Rudolf Dreikurs, a psychiatrist and author, has identi-fied four important principles for handling conflict.**

1. **Maintain mutual respect.** Avoid fighting *or* giving in.

   • Use reflective listening and I-messages. Show the other person you clearly understand: "I'm sensing you're feeling . . ."

   • Talk straight to him or her, making sure the person understands you: "I also want you to understand how I feel when this happens. When _____, I feel _____, because _____."

2. **Identify the real issue.** You may be discussing sharing responsibilities or the appropriate way to discipline. But what's being discussed is seldom the real issue. In a con-flict, many times the real issue is who's right, who's in charge, or one of fairness. You can say something like, "It seems to me we're both interested in being right. I wonder how this will help us solve the problem?"

---

*   Don Dinkmeyer et al., *The Effective Parent* (Circle Pines, MN: American Guidance Service, 1987), pp. 113-14.
** Rudolf Dreikurs and Loren Grey, *A Parent's Guide to Child Discipline* (New York: Hawthorn, 1970), pp. 42-43.

3. **Change the agreement.** In a conflict, the persons involved have made an agreement to quarrel. You can change the agreement by changing your own behavior. Be willing to compromise if necessary. "I'm aware we've been at odds over this and I'm willing to listen and attempt to reach agreement."

4. **Invite participation in decision making.** An agreement comes when both people suggest solutions and settle on one that both are willing to accept. This involves the brainstorming process. Begin the process by asking the other person for ideas. "How do you think we can solve this?" Then add your own ideas if necessary and proceed to considering solutions and attempting to arrive at, and commit to, a mutually agreeable solution.

   If agreement is not reached, all you can do is state your intentions: "Since we aren't willing to find a solution acceptable to both of us, then I choose to (state your intentions)." Your intentions simply tell what you will do—not what the other person is to do.

   If you have a conflict in your adult relationships you'd like to resolve, decide how to use the steps for exploring alternatives and the principles of conflict resolution to handle the conflict. How will you begin the discussion?

Chapter 4
Cooperation and Discipline

What You Will Learn

- Effective discipline is guidance that helps children learn self-control and cooperation.

- Effective ways of guiding children include using natural and logical consequences and giving them choices.

- Reward, punishment, and requiring unthinking obedience are not effective methods of discipline.

Guiding Children in Developing Self-Discipline

In selecting an appropriate method of discipline, it's important to consider a child's developmental level and any circumstances or goals that may be affecting behavior.

The children in our care are growing up to be part of a larger world. As members of groups and communities, they will need to know how to interact and cooperate with others. Learning these skills is one of the most important tasks of early childhood. This chapter is about helping children develop cooperative attitudes and skills.

Cooperative attitudes and behavior develop gradually over time. Through our model, children can begin to understand what cooperating means. We model cooperative behavior when we listen and show respect for other adults and the children in our program. By acknowledging children when they are cooperative, you encourage similar behavior in them.

Chapter 4 also deals with discipline. Discipline is guidance. Through helpful and respectful methods we teach cooperation, responsibility, and the development of self-discipline in children.

Realistic expectations, mutual respect, encouragement, communication skills—all help build cooperation and responsibility in young children.

What Is Cooperation?

Adults often use the word "cooperate" when they really mean "obey."

Three-year-olds Sabrina and Pamela are arguing about a doll. Each claims possession and says that she "had it first." The teacher is trying to listen to Vernon's story. She asks the girls to be quiet. They settle for awhile, but then continue their argument. Finally the teacher demands, "I want you two to cooperate! Stop that arguing or I will separate you!"

Although the teacher wants cooperation, it's obvious what she *really* wants is for the two girls to *obey*. Demanding obedience may make children do what we want—for awhile. But cooperation is not developed through demanding. Instead, this approach often produces rebellion. *Cooperation means working together to meet the needs of a particular situation,* not blind obedience.

In the situation with Sabrina and Pamela, the teacher could let the girls own the problem, and ask them to go to the Talk-It-Over Place to settle it. In this way the teacher helps the girls learn to cooperate with each other and the teacher. See Chapter 3 for information on using a Talk-It-Over Place.

Here's an example of group cooperation:

A kindergarten class is going to decorate their room for the holidays. They decide to make paper chains. After planning with the teacher and reviewing how to make the chains, the teacher asks what materials they'll need and who will volunteer to get them. If the children fail to understand what's needed, the teacher might ask, "Who wants to get the construction paper?" and so on.

There are many ways to help children learn cooperative attitudes and behavior. We want to use methods that both encourage positive behavior and discourage negative behavior.

How Much Cooperation Can You Expect?

Cooperation is something that grows gradually. Children's ability to cooperate is related to where they are in the development process. A child's movement toward independence may come into conflict with his ability to cooperate. It is up to the adults in children's lives to help them with both tasks—becoming independent *and* learning to cooperate with others.

Let's consider what kind of cooperation we can expect from infants, toddlers, and preschoolers. We'll also look at methods that can be effective in helping them develop cooperative behavior.

Infants. Infants are explorers. Every setting is new territory to explore. Infants discover things with all their senses—sight, hearing, smell, touch, taste. Because they are babies, they are explorers without rules or common sense. Therefore, *setting boundaries is the most loving and effective form of discipline for babies.*

Infants see themselves as the center of the universe. They have no understanding of the needs and rights of others. Because of this, babies can't be expected to cooperate naturally. But infancy is the perfect time to begin teaching cooperation. During children's first year, every interaction with them is a chance to show mutual respect and to encourage cooperation.

> *Eight-month-old Oralee has spit up all over herself. As the teacher cleans her she says, "Let's get you cleaned up. Here, you can help me." She puts the child's hand on the cloth and guides it over part of the soiled area.*

The child won't necessarily understand and cooperate. Oralee may pull her hand away. Babies are very determined, but they never intend to manipulate. Their behavior simply reflects their attempts to communicate their needs. Because of this, we don't consider their behavior negative—just naturally immature.

Toddlers. Toddlers like to explore, too. They are becoming aware of cause and effect in their actions: "When I scream, you cringe. When I cry, you hug." Toddlers start being able to predict the consequences of their behavior. They learn to change their behavior in order to change the consequences. Most toddlers have learned how to get an emotional rise out of their parents, so they may try it on you, too. A mischievous look in a toddler's eyes will tell you if his purpose is to test limits!

Toddlers need protective boundaries—maybe even more so than infants. They can move faster and farther than babies, but they don't have much self-control, and they don't recognize dangers. Although they continue to need clear physical boundaries, toddlers also need to learn social boundaries. They can begin to understand messages about what is and is not acceptable behavior.

Toddlers have a simplistic sense of what it means to cooperate. They often act in ways that appear totally uncooperative. Self-assertion is part of learning to become independent. It helps tod-

When we reward or punish children, we teach them to look to an <u>adult</u> to be responsible for their behavior. It is possible to influence cooperation without rewarding and punishing.

dlers develop self-esteem. But self-assertion may also bring the first signs of what is called *negativism*. Because the toddler is learning that she has control over herself, she may refuse to do what is asked, or may do the opposite. She may close her mouth firmly when you are trying to give her the last bite of food. She may run away when you are trying to button her coat. She is learning to say "No!"—loudly and often. The toddler is not being hostile. She's just learning what she can and can't do as she moves toward independence.

Effective discipline is guidance. It is a teaching and learning process. The goal of discipline is to help children develop self-discipline.

Psychologist Fitzhugh Dodson describes negativism as a passing phase between babyhood and early childhood. Without it, a child might remain stuck in babyhood. Handled appropriately, it can be a positive phase in a child's development.[1]

You can deal with negativism by helping redirect toddlers to positive activities that build independence and self-esteem. These are activities at which toddlers can succeed and for which they can be recognized. Recognizing positive behavior helps to build cooperation.

> *After splashing outside in some rain puddles, the toddler class comes in with wet feet. While the assistant teacher finds their dry socks, the head teacher says, "Help me by pulling off your wet socks. Your feet will feel much more comfortable. Look at your funny toes wiggling!"*

Preschoolers. Preschoolers are better able than toddlers to predict the consequences of their behavior and to use some degree of self-control. They have some ability to change their behavior to avoid unwanted consequences.

> *Three-year-old Sheila is washing the dolls in the water table in the four-year-old-room. Mary comes over to join in, but the girls have different ideas about how the game should go. Soon Mary has taken all the dolls away from Sheila. Sheila says, "I was here first!" and tries to shove Mary away. The teacher says, "Playing with the babies in the water is fun. Can you think of a way to do it together?" Sheila says,"I want to wash the babies." Mary says, "I want to wash their hair." Sheila responds, "Okay, I'll give them a bath. You wash their hair. Then we'll dry them."*

Because preschoolers can be more rational, they can be given clear, simple rules and the consequences for breaking them. They won't understand your expectations every time, or in every situation, but their understanding is growing.

> *The three-year-old group is using a parachute for the first time. The teacher explains that in order for parachute play to work, all the children need to hold tight to the edges and lift the parachute up and down at the same time. The teacher stresses that this will take lots of cooperation. Some of the children have trouble understanding what to do, so the teacher has several children who do understand demonstrate how to hold and lift the parachute.*

Effective Discipline

Realistic expectations, mutual respect, encouragement, communication skills—all help build cooperation and responsibility in young children. Within this framework, teachers can find effective methods of discipline. Effective discipline helps guide children in learning how to cooperate with others—and how to manage their own behavior.

Ineffective Methods: Reward and Punishment

Discipline is an educational process—a learning experience. But for some adults, *discipline* may mean punishment. Many of us were raised in families in which punishment—and its counterpart, reward—were the methods used to discipline children. But these methods don't offer children the chance to make choices so they can learn responsibility. Reward and punishment may seem effective when children are young. But they are methods that can have undesirable long-term consequences.

105

Rewards. Rewards teach children that they can expect payment for their cooperation.

- "If you're really good, I'll read you a story."

- "The first one to put on his jacket and boots gets a treat."

By relying on rewards, we train children to behave in a certain way in order to get something—not in order to cooperate. The rewards must increase in value as the child grows older. What motivates a two-year-old may not motivate a five-year-old. And because rewards tend to compare children with one another, they can set the stage for competition rather than cooperation.

Punishment. While rewards teach children to *get*, punishment teaches children to *resent*. Punishment guarantees a relationship based on fear. It is an attack on a child's self-esteem and it usually invites rebellion. Punishment may involve:

- Threats—which teachers often may not carry out. *"If you don't help clean up today, I won't let you play with the paints tomorrow."*

- Yelling—which often teaches children not to pay attention unless teachers scream. *"I've HAD IT with your fighting! Go sit on the time-out chair!"*

- Overreaction—which may make problems worse by magnifying their importance. *"You ripped a page of that book! No more books for you!"*

- Put-downs—which include insults, name calling, accusations, and unfavorable comparisons to other children. *"You guys are nothing but troublemakers."*

- Withdrawal of privileges that have no clear relationship to the misbehavior—which creates resentment. *"You made a mess in the bathroom, so you can't go outside at recess time."*

- Spanking—Spanking, hitting, or shaking children shows them that it's all right to use physical force to solve problems—especially if you're bigger! Giving children physical pain only teaches them to be afraid of adults. While spanking may stop misbehavior for awhile, in time it loses its effect as a way to teach and control behavior. Spanking may relieve an adult's anger, but most adults feel guilty afterward. Some children learn to use this guilt to get all sorts of privileges after a spanking. (And the use of corporal punishment in public schools is illegal in many states.)

When we reward or punish children, we teach them to look to an *adult* to be responsible for their behavior. It is possible to influence cooperation without rewarding and punishing.

Methods of Effective Discipline

Effective discipline is guidance. It is a teaching and learning process. The goal of discipline is to help children develop self-discipline—enabling them to be cooperative and responsible for their own behavior.

Children respond to respect and positive expectations. The keys to effective discipline are *establishing mutual respect and expecting cooperation.* The following methods can be used for effective discipline:

- **D**istracting children

- **I**gnoring misbehavior when appropriate

- **S**tructuring the environment

- **C**ontrolling the situation, not the child

- **I**nvolving children through choices and consequences

- **P**lanning time for loving and learning

- **L**etting go

- **I**ncreasing your consistency

- **N**oticing positive behavior

- **E**xcusing a child with a time-out

Methods of Effective Discipline

It's important to consider the child's developmental level when selecting a method of discipline. Distraction, for example, is a useful strategy with infants, while a time-out would be meaningless at this age. As a teacher, you must be knowledgeable about the developmental level and personality of each child in your care. While a particular technique may be appropriate for most children of a certain age, it may not be effective with a specific child. For example, you may discover that one of your preschoolers doesn't respond to I-messages.

You will also need to take into account factors in the child's life which may be affecting his behavior. Does he appear to be getting enough sleep? What's happening at home—has there been a change in the family? Factors like these will influence your choice of a discipline procedure. A child who is upset over a disruption at home, for example, may need extra cuddling during displays of uncooperative behavior, or encouraging words during transition times. If the behavior continues as a consistent pattern, you may need to contact the child's family. You'll want to be able to work together with them, if possible, to help the child manage his behavior.

With misbehavior, you'll need to understand this child's goal. Ignoring may be effective with a child who disturbs in order to gain attention. But a child seeking power may need to be removed from the situation.

Distracting Children

Remember, we are ignoring the behavior, not the child.

> *Eleven-month-old Sao pounds seven-month-old Bonnie quite hard. Sao's teacher hands him a drum and gently says, "Here, Sao, we bang on drums, not people."*

In this situation, the teacher uses an important skill of effective discipline—*distracting*. She does not scold him, but rather offers him an alternative. She then explains what's permissible.

> *If Sao continues his rough handling of Bonnie, his teacher might pick him up and move him to another area of the room. If he continues to crawl back and attack Bonnie, a solution might be to hold him in her lap for a little while. This is all done in a friendly, non-threatening manner. Later, the teacher might help Sao practice gentle touches.*

Distraction works well with younger babies too. It deals with their eager curiosity and short attention span in a respectful way. If you're holding a baby and he suddenly pulls off your glasses, give him something else to play with.

Ignoring Misbehavior When Appropriate

Ignoring can be used to handle minor disturbances that are not destructive or dangerous—such as constant talking, showing off, sulking, whining, mild crying, temper tantrums, power plays, attempts to interrupt or beg for treats, and insults.

> *Three-year-old Jay is a non-stop talker. Once he gets started it's hard to get him to stop. The teacher, Tom, decides to set some limits on Jay's talking behavior. He tells Jay, "I have just a minute to listen to what you have to say, then I need to work with the other children." He gives Jay his full attention for one minute. Then Tom states that he'll talk with Jay later, but now he needs to be with the others. The teacher busies himself with another group. Jay tags along talking for awhile, but Tom is effectively ignoring him, and Jay eventually gives it up.*

In some situations, it can be ineffective to ignore misbehavior—for example, with a child whose showing off is disturbing the group. In this case, you might decide to excuse the child from the group for awhile until she's ready to participate cooperatively.

Ignoring can be an effective discipline method.

Ignoring misbehavior involves more than not talking to the child who's misbehaving. If you still communicate your feelings by your facial expression or body language, children will know you're not really ignoring them. You can help yourself really ignore a child by busying yourself with other children. Realize the child's misbehavior may get worse before it gets better—most children don't give up easily. But your persistence will usually pay off.

Ignoring a behavior is an effective way to discourage it. Remember, we are ignoring the behavior, not the child. When a child behaves appropriately, give the child attention—encouraging the child, without reinforcing a negative goal.

Structuring the Environment

To learn, young children need to be free to explore most spaces and objects in their environment. A well-structured environment prevents many problems and promotes learning. Verna Hildebrand, author of *Guiding Young Children*, suggests if you're looking for a solution to a behavior problem, check the structure of the environment first.[2]

Lunchtime is stressful in the infant room. All the children want attention simultaneously. The staff decides to divide the class into two groups, and have two staff members feed some of the infants while the third staff member plays tapes or musical instruments for the other babies. The infants are fascinated by the instruments, and the music seems to have a soothing effect on everyone.

It's up to us to structure the environment so children can have more hands-on than hands-off experiences. If a child chooses to do something destructive or dangerous, teachers can use distraction, remove the "off-limits" item, limit the space for free exploration, or remove the child if necessary. By limiting the need to say no, we create a more cooperative atmosphere for children. Careful structuring ahead of time can go a long way toward lessening instances of misbehavior.

It's up to us to structure the environment so children can have more hands-on than hands-off experiences.

Structure the environment for more hands-on than hands-off experiences.

There are three types of environmental structuring.[3] We need to structure for:

• Safety

• Cooperation

• Learning

Safety. A safe environment minimizes accidents and gives children room to roam. Do you have safety plugs in electric outlets? Are other dangerous objects put away or blocked off? Are toys durable, without small pieces which may break and injure children?

Cooperation. Learning requires cooperation—between adults and children, and among children. Here are some examples of structuring for cooperation:

Mrs. Whitefoot knows that older babies need variety in their playthings. She also knows that crawlers and early walkers have a tendency to clear the shelves and dump everything onto the floor. There are three low, open shelves in Mrs. Whitefoot's classroom. She chooses to put several toys on each shelf and rotate the toys weekly from a larger supply kept in a cupboard with doors. This way, the babies are continually exposed to, and challenged by, new materials without cleanup being a major headache for the staff.

Ms. Fuller notices that the toddlers have trouble sharing and taking turns, because they are so young. Her director offers her a chance to order new materials. Ms. Fuller decides to order duplicates of the favorite toys so that there will be less need to share. She knows the toddlers will eventually learn to share, but she also understands that they aren't developmentally ready for sharing yet.

In the three-year-old room, the art area is on the opposite side of the room from the sink. Children with paint on their hands are continually touching things as they leave the art table to go to the sink. The teacher decides to move the art table next to the sink.

Learning. Children under six need plenty of concrete and relevant experiences.[4] Providing a balance of interesting activities is the most effective way to prevent discipline problems and encourage cooperation. We need to provide:

- time together for stories and sharing.

- time for the children to explore alone and in learning centers.

- time for both inside and outside activities.[5]

The way to provide for the needs of both children and adults is for adults to control the situation by setting guidelines and giving children freedom to choose within those boundaries.

Structuring for Learning

Infants. Allow babies to follow their own schedules for eating, sleeping, and playing. Provide objects they can see, feel, and chew. Crib mobiles, posters, and mirrors placed at their eye level will give visual interest. Infants who can move around need safe spaces to crawl and explore—both indoors and out. Outside areas need climbing and crawling structures with different textures and surfaces.[6]

Toddlers. Toddlers are fast moving and need constant supervision. Accidents and aggressive behavior can happen in an instant. Toddlers like to run, jump, hop, climb, and manipulate objects. They like to play in water, sand, and clay. Toddlers benefit from a routine they can depend on, with familiar events that follow a pattern. For example, singing comes before lunch, snacks follow naptime.[7]

Preschoolers. Many of the suggestions for toddlers also apply to preschoolers. Preschoolers, though, are more mature and will need an environment suited to their expanding capabilities. Young preschoolers—three-year-olds—need more close supervision than older ones. Preschoolers aren't able to sit for long periods of time, but four- and five-year-olds will be interested in a group time longer than three-year-olds.[8]

Controlling the Situation, Not the Child

Teachers may worry that unless they control a child, the child will control them. Yet most children, just like adults, want to feel that they have some real control in their own lives. *The way to provide for the needs of both children and adults is for adults to control the situation by setting guidelines and giving children freedom to choose within those boundaries.* This gives children control—they have a real choice, within the limits we've set. We're not controlling children by telling them what they must do—we're controlling the situation and encouraging them to make choices for themselves. When we let children control aspects of their lives that are appropriate for their developmental level, we're more likely to see greater cooperation even at times when their choices are more limited.[9]

With older toddlers and preschoolers, state the limits and ask the children to choose:

- "You may play together as long as there is no fighting. You decide."

If the children start fighting again, say:

- "I see you have decided not to play together for awhile."

> *The children in the kindergarten housekeeping area have been cleaning up by just stuffing items anywhere. The teacher says to the five-year-olds, "You need to pick up carefully or else not play here. Let's cooperate to clean up." She helps the children put pictures of pots and pans on the play stove, food on the play refrigerator, and dishes and cups on the dish cupboard. The next day, the children carefully match the playthings to the pictures at cleanup time.*

Involving Children Through Choices and Consequences

As children grow, we want them to learn to make decisions and take responsibility for their own behavior. Giving choices to young children helps them begin to develop independence and cooperation. You can give simple choices to children that respect their desire for control and help you keep order at the same time:

- "Which puzzle would you like to play with?"

- "Do you want the rattle or the teddy bear?" (Pause and let the infant reach for what she wants.)

In a situation with choices, a child may say, "No, I want this!" Your reply can be, "That's not one of the choices."

A similar approach can be taken when a child keeps changing his mind. For example, Danny chooses one toy, then changes his mind and wants the toy Alice has. That's not one of the choices because the other toy is already being used.

Attending to children's positive efforts shows them you care. Children who feel loved and appreciated will be more inclined to be cooperative. Showing love builds self-esteem.

> *The teacher asks, "Would you rather have apple juice or pear juice?" Once two-year-old Jeremy chooses apple juice and starts to drink out of the carton, the choice has been made.*

Natural and Logical Consequences
When a toddler's or preschooler's behavior needs correction, you can use natural and logical consequences.[10]

Natural Consequences. *Natural consequences result from going against the laws of nature.* The child who refuses to eat

As children gain confidence in themselves and learn to cooperate, we can show our confidence in them by learning to let go.

lunch will soon get hungry. Wet clothes that a child refuses to change may become increasingly uncomfortable to wear.

Natural consequences are effective without any action from adults.

Five-year-old Beth refuses to put on her mittens before outdoor playtime. Her teacher remarks, "It's cold outside," but decides not to make it into a power struggle. Outside, Beth's hands get cold. She has to keep them in her pockets, and isn't able to join in playground fun.

Natural consequences aren't always the best way to correct a child's behavior. Many situations don't have natural consequences. And some natural consequences are dangerous. For example, in a very cold climate a child might get frostbite going outdoors to play without mittens. In that case, natural consequences are not appropriate. The teacher must set up logical consequences.

Another place for caution with natural consequences is the use of outdoor play equipment. We wouldn't let a two-and-a-half-year-old stand on the swing and fall off so he won't do it again! Instead, we set up a logical consequence: "You could fall and hurt yourself. Do you want to get down on your own or shall I help you down?"

If the child won't come down on his own, the teacher would gently remove him from the swing. If the child tried to climb on the swing again, the teacher would remove him and give him another choice: "You may play here as long as you use the swing safely and sit down on it instead of standing."

If the behavior continues, assume he has chosen to play in another area for awhile.

Logical Consequences. *Logical consequences are the result of going against the rules of social cooperation.* They reflect the needs of a particular situation.

> *In the three-year-old room, Suzanne throws blocks at Pedro because she doesn't want him in the block area. The teacher says, "Suzanne, blocks are for building, not throwing. If you want to stay in the block area, you'll need to stop throwing blocks." A few minutes later, Suzanne throws blocks again. The teacher removes her from the block area to another part of the room, saying, "Suzanne, you're still throwing blocks. That tells me you've decided not to play in the block area right now. Where would you like to play instead?" If Suzanne decides to play in the block area later in the day, it will be important that the same rule, blocks are not for throwing, still apply.*

Logical consequences have the following characteristics:

1. They express the rules of social living.

> *Three-year-old Luisa refuses to share her huge ball of Play-Doh with another child, Matt. Matt leaves and decides to play in the housekeeping area with some other children. A moment later, Luisa is complaining that she's lonely and "no one wants to play with me." Her teacher respectfully says to her, "Other children don't like to play when you don't share. If you share, we can ask Matt to give you another chance."*

2. They are related to the misbehavior.

> *Two-year-old Jesse dumps out his juice and crumbles his crackers on the table. Jesse's teacher hands him a sponge and helps him clean up his mess. Jesse learns if he makes a mess, he must clean it up. Scolding Jesse or putting him on a time-out chair would not relate to the misbehavior.*

3. They separate the deed from the doer. Logical consequences don't imply a child is bad because the child is misbehaving. Instead, they communicate, "While I don't like what you're doing, I still like you."

> *Three-year-old Jamica rips a page in a book while turning pages carelessly. Jamica's teacher doesn't call her careless, but she does expect Jamica to help tape the page back together. She tells Jamica, "We need to get some tape and tape it back together."*

When we show faith and confidence that children can handle challenges appropriate to their ages and maturity, we build children's belief in themselves.

4. They are concerned with what will happen now. Logical consequences are for dealing with the present—not with past misbehavior. This sets the stage for what happens today.

> *After being removed from the water table earlier for splashing and making a mess, four-year-old Brian's teacher allows him to try again. She reminds him of her expectations by saying, "Brian, please show me how you're going to keep the water in the tub. What can you do with the water pump?"*

5. They are given in a friendly way. With logical consequences, teachers can stress mutual respect by using a tone of voice and nonverbal behavior that show firmness and friendliness at the same time.

> *Two-and-a-half-year-old Margie is dawdling on her way into the nap room. Her teacher says, "Margie, you need to go to your cot now. Would you like to walk to the nap room, or shall I carry you?"*

Children need discipline that is consistent. When teachers consistently treat the same behavior in the same way, children will know what to expect if they misbehave.

6. They permit choice. With choice, children have the chance to choose responsible behavior rather than being told how to behave.

> *"You can play in the sandbox as long as you dig. If you throw sand at someone else, you'll need to leave the sandbox."*

Infants and Consequences

In most cases, logical consequences are not appropriate in dealing with infants' behavior. Babies aren't yet able to think logically or to understand cause-effect relationships.

Guidelines for Using Logical Consequences

Following a few guidelines can help make consequences work effectively:

Let the child's decision stand. When a child makes a choice let the decision stand—for the moment. Later, give the child another chance to show she is ready to cooperate.

> *The four-year-olds are putting on their swimsuits to splash in the wading pool. Denise decides not to put on her swimsuit and says she wants to ride the tricycle instead. While she's riding, Denise sees her friends in the pool and starts yelling because she wants to join them. Her teacher says, "I'm sorry Denise. You chose to ride the tricycle today, and you don't have your swimsuit on. The time is almost up anyway. Tomorrow you can choose the pool if you wish."*

With repeated misbehavior, increase the time of the consequence. Each time the same misbehavior occurs, increase the amount of time for the consequence. This will reinforce the message and the child will begin to understand the need for cooperation.

> *Three-and-a-half-year-old Troy paints on the wall instead of the easel for the second day in a row. Yesterday, his teacher had him help clean off the paint. But today, he's still not ready to follow the rules. His teacher decides that in addition to helping clean up, he'll lose his right to paint at the easel the following day.*

Phrase the choice respectfully. Use a friendly and helpful tone. One way to phrase a consequence is to say:

- "You may put on a smock to paint, or choose something else. You decide."

- To the group: "You may quiet down and we'll have a story, or else we can't have a story today. You decide."

Another way is to say, "You may_____ if you_____."

- "You may paint, if you put on a smock."

- To the group: "We can have a story, if there is quiet."

A statement of your intentions or assumptions is also a logical consequence. It gives the child a choice about how to respond.

- "I'll help you if you ask me nicely."

- "If you don't have your coat on by the time the others are finished leaving, I'll assume you don't want to go outside today."

Respect the child's choice. Children will often choose the consequence to see if you mean what you say. This is the way they learn the limits. You can respect the child's choice by making a simple statement.

- "I see you've decided."

117

You and Your Relationships

Noticing positive behavior can be effective in adult relationships too. A quiet comment that recognizes someone's positive contribution, helpful gesture, or skill, will be appreciated and remembered long after you say it.

Paying positive attention to the contributions of others gives people the morale-building knowledge that their work is noticed, and that their efforts are valued. Coworkers, spouses, and friends can all benefit from this kind of attention.

- "Your behavior tells me you've decided."

Tell the child when he can have another chance to show that he's ready to cooperate: "You may try again (state when)."

Say as little as possible. Talking too much reinforces children's misbehavior goals. Say only what needs to be said, and then simply act. Avoid nagging or threatening. The goal of letting children choose is to allow them to learn from their own experiences.

Make it clear when there's no choice. Giving a choice when there really is no choice sets the stage for problems. The same is true for open-ended choices. If, when it's time for a child to come inside, you ask, "Do you want to come in now?" you'll probably get a no. Instead, simply state, "It's time to come in now."

If a child balks, give him a choice of how he wants to come in: "Do you want to come in on your own, or shall I help you?" Watch his behavior, and act on his decision.

Keep hostility out of your consequences. If teachers communicate hostility in any way, they'll turn consequences into punishment. Keep calm. Be both kind and firm—at the same time. Show respect for yourself and the children. Work on your feelings. (See "Just For You" at the end of this chapter.)

Planning Time for Loving and Learning

Attending to children's positive efforts shows them you care. Children who feel loved and appreciated will be more inclined to be cooperative. Showing love builds self-esteem.

In the infant room, the teachers and aides take time to cuddle and talk with the children after feeding them.

In the toddler room, when the children have all settled down for their naps, the teacher softly sings a song that includes the name of each child as part of the daily routine.

In the four-year-old room, the teacher has a routine to make sure everyone gets a chance to talk about the day and get listened to. At lunchtime, the staff person at each table asks each child to tell the other children what he did that morning. Each child gets a chance to describe his accomplishments.

In the kindergarten room, each child has a special day of her own. The child brings photos, favorite toys, and collections from home to share. The designated child gets to choose the story and song for the day. The staff tells the child things that are special about him or her. They write these unique qualities on a poster and put it beside the picture of the child.

All children need and want attention. But it is not possible or desirable to attend to *everything* each child does—either positive or negative. Giving children attention every time they ask for it gives them an unrealistic picture of life.

Still, we need to find time to pay attention to children's positive efforts to contribute. One way of doing this is to use a checklist of the children in your group to see how often you give attention to each one. Next to each child's name, check each time you have given that child positive attention. In this way, you can see if there are some children you don't give as much attention to— perhaps because they don't ask for a lot of attention. With a checklist, you can make plans and track your progress.

Letting Go

As children gain confidence in themselves and learn to cooperate, we can show our confidence in them by learning to let go. When we show faith and confidence that children can handle challenges appropriate to their ages and maturity, we build children's belief in themselves. Letting go at appropriate times and in appropriate ways is one way we help children do this.

The more time you spend on noticing and commenting on positve behavior, the less time you'll have to spend correcting negative behavior.

> *On the playground two-and-a-half-year-old Jamie calls to the teacher. Flushed and happy, Jamie is hanging on tightly near the top of the climber. Instead of lifting Jamie down with cautious and discouraging words, the teacher smiles at Jamie's excitement and asks, "Can you climb down, too? Let's see how you do it!"*
>
> ---
>
> *Five-year-old Irma uses a wheelchair and wears leg braces. The teachers were concerned about how she'd manage at large muscle exercise time, but Irma's parents encouraged the teachers to let her move at her own pace. Within several weeks, Irma was engaged in relay races up and down the length of the gym with her friends. The children confided to their teachers, "Irma's really fast! It's fun to race with her."*

Time-out is a way to help a toddler or preschooler regain self-control. The procedure excuses the child temporarily from interacting with others and provides time for the child to calm down.

It can be hard to let children stand on their own if we give, or expect, too much in certain areas:

Overprotection. Children need protection, yet overprotection leads to a lack of self-confidence. Some examples of overprotection are:

- Settling children's relationship problems for them, rather than teaching them skills for solving their own problems.

- Protecting children from the logical consequences of their behavior—by lecturing, reminding, overlooking, or not following through.

Obedience. We don't help children, or ourselves, by trying to produce robots who obey our every wish. Children treated this way may become resentful and rebellious. Instead, we can offer choices within limits, and let children learn from their own decisions.

Permissiveness. Letting go doesn't mean teachers should let children do whatever they please. When we are too permissive, we teach children they have a right to get whatever they want, regardless of the rights of others. Ask yourself, "Will permitting this behavior help the children learn to cooperate with others?" If the answer is no, you'll want to set limits on the behavior.

Increasing Your Consistency

Children need discipline that is consistent. When teachers consistently treat the same behavior in the same way, children will know what to expect if they misbehave. If you're inconsistent, children will learn to read your moods rather than to cooperate.

Work to increase your consistency, but also accept your limitations. No human being is ever completely consistent.

Noticing Positive Behavior

It's easy to spend a lot of time focusing on children's negative behavior. But focusing on negative behavior teaches children that misbehaving is an effective way to belong. It's better to teach them that positive cooperation produces a happier kind of belonging.

Positive interactions support children's self-image and confidence, and can help prevent misbehavior. We can notice when children are cooperating with others: "Ewan, it looks like you and Malcolm are getting that road built fast together."

It's especially helpful to comment on positive behavior soon after you've had to correct misbehavior. That helps children learn you've rejected their behavior, but not them: "Looks like you're having fun taking turns at playing lotto."

By noticing children's positive behavior, we can give them more yes responses than no responses. Limits are necessary, but we can balance them with effective, positive interactions with children.[11] An important point to keep in mind is: *The more time you spend on noticing and commenting on positive behavior, the less time you'll have to spend correcting negative behavior.*

Excusing the Child with a Time-Out

Time-out is a way to help a toddler or preschooler regain self-control. The procedure *excuses* the child temporarily from interacting with others and provides time for the child to calm down.

When a tantrum gets out of control, you'll have to intervene.

A time-out is appropriate only for very disruptive behaviors:

- Temper tantrums that can't be ignored, are very disruptive to the group, and are designed to punish or make you or other children give in.

- Constant interference with others' activities that can't be ignored, such as interrupting your interaction with another child or disturbing the group.

- Violent acts by a toddler or a preschooler, such as hitting or biting. Young children don't usually resort to aggressive behaviors out of malice. More often, especially if the child is not very verbal, aggressive acts may be the only way the child knows how to communicate strong feelings. A time-out may be used to stop the immediate behavior. Later, help the child learn more words for feelings. This may help the child change physically aggressive behavior in the future.[12]

Time-out can be presented as a *choice*. A child can choose to settle down or take some time out. Used appropriately, *a time-out is a form of logical consequences.* It has two purposes:

- To teach a child he can learn to control his behavior if he wants to be around others.

- To give you and the group a chance to gain control of your own behavior and emotions.

The most effective time-out is for the child to lose her "audience." This could mean you and the group move away from the disruptive child—leaving her by herself. When this is ineffective or impractical and you have to remove the child, follow these guidelines:

Select a location for the time-out. Call the area the Calm-Down Place. An indoor Calm-Down Place should be away from activity areas—perhaps behind a screen. Make the area comfortable and suitable for calming down. Decorate the area with colors and pictures that suggest calmness. A large stuffed animal or bean bag chair could be there for snuggling up to, or for punching, if a child decides to do that.

Sometimes children may go to the Calm-Down Place just to play quietly. That's okay. If you then need it for a child who's having difficulty, simply tell the playing child that another child needs to be by herself now, and ask him to please play in another part of the room for awhile.

Be positive.[13] *Remember that time-out is not designed to be a punishment.* The purpose of a time-out is simply to allow the child to gain self-control. With older preschoolers and kindergartners, explain the purpose of the Calm-Down Place to the group. You could say something like: "How many of you have times when you get really mad?" (Chances are you'll have several hands up on this!)

"We all get mad at times, and sometimes our mad behavior bothers others. It's okay to feel angry. When we do, we need some time to calm ourselves down. There is a place in the room where you can go to help yourself calm down. We call it the Calm-Down Place." (Show them the place.)

"So, if you're feeling real mad, you can go to the Calm-Down Place and stay for a few minutes until you feel better. Sometimes we get so mad we don't know we're bothering other people. When this happens, I'll give you a choice of calming down where you are, or going to the Calm-Down Place for a few minutes if you need to be by yourself for awhile."

With younger preschoolers and toddlers, you'll need to explain the procedure to the individual child who needs to calm down. When possible, it's best to give this information before a problem arises. Take the child to the area and say something like, "Aaron, this is the Calm-Down Place. Sometimes you scream and it bothers us. So if you scream, I'll ask you to come here until you can be quiet."

The next time Aaron throws a tantrum that's bothering others, ask him if he wants to calm down now, or go to the Calm-Down Place until he's ready to play again. If his behavior shows he needs some time out, take him to the Calm-Down Place, and tell him you'll come back in a few minutes to see if he's ready to return to the group.

Plan an appropriate length of time. As much as possible, allow children to take the time they need without setting specific limits. Be clear about what kind of behavior you expect in order for the child to return to the group: "When you're done crying, you may come back and listen to the story with us." This encourages the child to develop internal control.

If you need to set time limits, two or three minutes is plenty the first time. If the behavior continues after the child returns to the group, add a minute for each new time-out. Usually, make five minutes a maximum—that's a long time to a young child, even a five-year-old. Also, if the child doesn't want to return to the group, that's okay too.

When a time-out is over, it's over. There's no need to discuss it. That would only call attention to the behavior you want to stop.

Discipline Is Guidance

Effective discipline is teaching cooperation. As with any interaction with children, patience and understanding—along with a sense of humor—will help see you through. If you keep in mind the purpose of discipline—to guide children to develop self-discipline—you'll keep a realistic perspective. Your helpful, respectful methods will offer children many positive models for dealing with problems.

Notes

1. Fitzhugh Dodson, *How to Parent* (New York: New American Library, 1973).

2. Verna Hildebrand, *Guiding Young Children (4th ed.)* (New York: Macmillan, 1990), p. 24.

3. For more discussion of structuring the environment, see:

Sue Bredekamp, ed., *Developmentally Appropriate Practice in Early Childhood Programs Serving Children from Birth to Age 8 (Expanded Edition)* (Washington, D.C.: National Association for the Education of Young Children, 1987), pp. 4, 10.

Stephanie Feeney, Doris Christensen, and Eva Moravcik, *Who Am I in the Lives of Children? (4th ed.)* (Columbus, OH: Merrill, 1991), pp. 188-89.

Beverly Gulley, E. Jacqueline Eddleman, and Douglas Bedient, *Training for Professional Child Care* (Carbondale and Edwardsville, IL: Southern Illinois University Press, 1987), p. 96.

Hildebrand, p. 24.

Eleanor Reynolds, *Guiding Young Children: A Child Centered Approach* (Mountain View, CA: Mayfield, 1990), p. 58.

Elaine Surbeck and Michael Kelley, eds., *Personalizing Care with Infants, Toddlers, and Families* (Wheaton, MD: Association for Childhood Education International, 1990), pp. 35-36.

4. Bredekamp, pp. 4, 10.

This book outlines the National Association for the Education of Young Children's (NAEYC) position on educating and caring for young children. It is an important resource for teachers of young children.

5. Gulley et al., p. 96.

6. Feeney, et al., pp. 188-89, and Reynolds, p. 58.

7. Surbeck and Kelley, pp. 35-36.

8. Bredekamp, pp. 4, 10.

9. Stanley Greenspan and Nancy Thorndike Greenspan, *First Feelings* (New York: Viking Penguin, 1985), p. 211.

10. Rudolf Dreikurs originated the concepts of natural and logical consequences. Rudolf Dreikurs and Vickie Soltz, *Children the Challenge* (New York: Hawthorn Books, 1964).

11. Greenspan and Greenspan, p. 141.

12. Hildebrand, pp. 293-295.

13. Jane Nelson and H. Stephen Glenn, *Time Out: Abuses and Effective Uses* (Provo, UT: Sunrise Press, 1991), p. 10.

Problem Situations

Infant. Eight-month-old Paula is fascinated by earrings. One of the older infants, Anna, has pierced ears with gold rings in them. Often Paula notices Anna's earrings, and her hands quickly grab and pull, causing Anna to shriek and one of the infant teachers to come running.

1. Is Paula misbehaving?

2. What can Paula's teacher do to discourage Paula's earring pulling?

Toddler. Corey, who is twenty months old, has a "wild" time of day nearly every morning before lunch. Typically Corey will begin to run around the block or doll corner pulling blocks, dolls, and doll clothes out of their baskets. He scatters them all over the floor, shrieking and laughing. When his teachers try to stop him, he'll often throw a tantrum.

1. What are some ways Corey's teacher might structure the environment to encourage more cooperative behavior from Corey?

2. What are some other discipline methods the teacher might consider if it's not possible to restructure the environment?

Preschooler. Four-and-a-half-year-old Julie has learned several swearwords which she uses around the other children in the four-year-old room. The other children laugh and mimic her. Recently, three parents complained to Julie's teacher that their children are picking up a lot of bad language at school.

1. What are some discipline methods other than ignoring that Julie's teacher might use in this situation?

2. Specifically, how could the teacher construct logical consequences to deal with the swearing?

Chart 4

Logical Consequences of Misbehavior*

Infants

Many problem behaviors of babies can be dealt with more easily when teachers understand the child's developmental needs and abilities. Infants need to explore in order to learn. Structure the environment so they can have more hands-on than hands-off experiences. Careful childproofing is a must for mobile infants.

Toddlers and Preschoolers

Toddlers and preschoolers also need an environment that allows for hands-on experiences and is still childproofed. Keep in mind that all young children need to be given clear guidelines and limits.

Misbehavior Example	Consequence Category	Logical Consequence
Child doesn't come to table for snack.	Denial or delay of activity	After setting a timer to denote the last five minutes of snack period, the timer goes off. Snacks are matter-of-factly removed and put away, with no after-snack-time exceptions.
Group doesn't put away toys.		Teacher leads cooperative cleanup, explaining that the time for outside play (or stories, or music), is being shortened because toys aren't picked up yet.
Demands attention.	Loss of involvement	Teacher ignores.
Disrupts group activity.		Child leaves group—possible time-out.
Handles an object inappropriately.	Denial of use of object	Show appropriate use. If misbehavior continues, deny use of toy temporarily.
Takes toy from another child.		Invite children to discuss problem. If child refuses, give choice: return toy to child who had it first, or you will.
Causes disturbance on field trip.	Denial of access to places	Teacher gently restrains child and says, "You forgot the rules about walking and talking quietly. I want you to stay next to me until I'm sure you are going to follow the rules."
Throws blocks in block area.		Don't allow child in area until she's ready.
Tries to interrupt.	Denial of cooperation	Teacher ignores interruptions or gives child choice of remaining silent until she's finished, or leaving area.
Demands help.		Help not given until child asks respectfully. If toddler is out of control with tantrum, help child calm down; then discuss.

*Adapted from Jerrold I. Gilbert, "Logical Consequences: A New Classification for the Classroom." Individual Psychology 454 (December, 1989) 425-432.

Applying Your Skills

This week practice applying discipline skills in guiding children's behavior choices in two or three specific instances. Identify several kinds of problem behavior ahead of time which you often encounter. Decide which discipline skills might be helpful in each situation.

The discipline skills discussed in this session of *TLC* were:

Distracting children.
Ignoring misbehavior when appropriate.
Structuring the environment.
Controlling the situation, not the child.
Involving children through choices and consequences.
Planning time for loving and learning.
Letting go.
Increasing your consistency.
Noticing positive behavior.
Excusing a child with a time-out.

Things to Consider

While these skills have been found to be effective in most cases, you will want to determine a skill's effectiveness in your situation. As you think about helping the children:

- Examine the child's environment in each situation—activities and scheduling factors which may be contributing to the problem.

- Examine any personal liabilities on your part, such as being easy to anger, talking too much, being demanding, having to be in control, trying to be perfect, wanting to please.

- Assess your personal resources for solving this problem. These are qualities or strengths such as a sense of humor, skill in problem solving, patience, or being perceptive.

Follow-Up

Your leader will provide time to discuss your results with the group at your next meeting. If your group does not meet again, plan a time to evaluate your efforts with others in your center who have taken the *TLC* class. If the results of the assignment are unsatisfactory, decide how you can change your approach in the future.

Record Keeping (Optional)

You may find it helpful to log your observations and actions. The following format can be used for your log.

Daily Log   Child's Name:_____

	Child's Behavior	Discipline Skill Used	Results
Monday			
Tuesday			
Wednesday			
Thursday			
Friday			

1. Cooperation means working together to meet the needs of a situation. Children develop attitudes and skills for cooperation gradually, over time.

2. Infants need physical boundaries. They can't naturally cooperate, but they can begin to learn about cooperation.

3. Toddlers need physical and social boundaries. They begin to assert themselves and may exhibit negativism—refusing to do what is asked or doing the opposite.

4. Preschoolers have some self-control. They can understand the consequences of their behavior and have some ability to learn from the consequences.

5. Effective discipline helps children learn self-control and cooperation.

6. Reward and punishment are not effective methods of discipline. They teach children to expect an adult to be responsible for their behavior.

7. In selecting an appropriate method, it's important to consider a child's developmental level and any factors in the child's life which may be affecting his behavior.

8. Effective methods of discipline are:
   - **D**istracting children.
   - **I**gnoring misbehavior when appropriate.
   - **S**tructuring the environment.
   - **C**ontrolling the situation, not the child.
   - **I**nvolving children through choices and consequences.
   - **P**lanning time for loving and learning.
   - **L**etting go.
   - **I**ncreasing your consistency.
   - **N**oticing positive behavior.
   - **E**xcusing a child with a time-out.

9. When looking for a solution to a behavior problem, check the structure of the environment first. An appropriate environment prevents many discipline problems. We need to structure for:
   - Safety
   - Cooperation
   - Learning

10. Natural and logical consequences can be used when children make inappropriate choices.
    - Natural consequences result from going against the laws of nature.
    - Logical consequences are the result of going against the rules of social cooperation.

11. Logical consequences:
    - express the rules of social living.
    - are related to the misbehavior.
    - separate the deed from the doer.
    - are concerned with what will happen now, not past behavior.
    - are given in a friendly way.
    - permit choice.

12. A time-out is a logical consequence. Use it only for very disruptive behaviors. Be positive—time-out is not designed to punish, just to allow a child to gain self-control.

Managing Your Feelings When Children Misbehave

Discipline is most effective when it is administered in a calm, rational manner. Negative emotions on our part reinforce children's misbehavior goals. Children will *expect* us to become annoyed, angry, hurt, or to feel despair when they misbehave.

Emotions are a form of energy. We use them as "fuel" for our behavior. If we want to move close to an individual, for example, we create warmth towards that person. If we want to distance ourselves from others, we may generate anger to create the distance. Emotions serve a purpose—fueling our action. Negative emotions can create distance and problems in relationships.

1. **Recognize the purpose of your emotional responses to children's misbehavior goals.** The first step for us in learning to keep emotions out of discipline is to recognize the purpose of our negative emotional responses to children's misbehavior goals.

   Attention. When children seek inappropriate attention, we may feel *annoyed*. The purpose of our annoyance is to get the child to stop seeking the attention. The annoyance gives us the energy to remind and coax the child.

   Power. Power seeking children can stimulate our *anger*. The purpose of our anger is to force compliance. By getting angry, we try to make the child do what we want, rather than just coax him, as we do when we get annoyed. Anger is a much more intense emotion.

   Revenge. When children seek revenge, we may feel *hurt*. We create the hurt to give ourselves permission to get even. Then we generate anger to carry out the retaliation. In this case, anger is used to wound.

   Display of Inadequacy. Children who display inadequacy invite us to feel *despair*—we want to give up. When we fall into deep discouragement or despair, we believe nothing can be done. The despair we create gives us permission to give up on the child.

When we respond to children out of the negative emotional purposes of annoyance, anger, hurt, or despair, we are *not* helping them. Our focus as teachers needs to stay on what is good for the child. What does he need? What are his goals? What will help him learn best in this situation? Maintaining this focus isn't always easy. How do we go about it?

2. **Manage your self-talk.** We create our emotions by what we tell ourselves. Absolute terms like: "It's awful." "I can't stand it!" "How dare you?" "You should (or must) do this." "You're a bad kid." "I'm a terrible teacher!"—all create strong, upset emotions. To be effective with children, we need to examine our self-talk and choose new ways of talking to ourselves in response to misbehavior goals.

Attention. When children seek attention, we may say to ourselves privately, "This kid's a nuisance," or, "Oh no, here she goes again—what a pain!" These phrases will lead to inner annoyance, no matter how calmly we seem to be reacting on the outside. Instead, say to yourself something like this: "She's after my attention—I'll ignore this behavior." Such a phrase will lead you directly to the action you need to take, and make it emotionally easier to do so.

Power. When you encounter a power seeker, you may think something like, "This child won't get away with that! He must and will do what I say! I'll show him who's boss!" Obviously, such inner talk will create anger. Instead, consider the situation—"He wants me to fight with him. I'll remain calm and refuse to fight."

Revenge. Children who get even invite strong, negative thinking on our part. That's the purpose of the revenge behavior. You may tell yourself, "How dare she say that to me! This is awful! I can't stand being talked to that way! I'll get her for this!" This talk will lead you to hurt and anger. Instead, you might say to yourself, "This child is hurt and wants to hurt in return. I'll show compassion instead of letting her hurt me."

Display of Inadequacy. A child who displays inadequacy invites you to give up. Your self-talk might be something like, "I've failed with this child, there's nothing I can do. How awful! I'm inadequate, and this child is beyond help." Despair will certainly result from this kind of talk! Instead, realize the child believes she's incapable because she is discouraged. The child's belief is not a testimony to your—or her—inadequacy. Tell yourself, "This child is very discouraged. I will not feel inadequate myself or give up on her! Instead, I will look for the slightest effort, and focus on it."

3. **Take notice of your feelings when children misbehave.** When you're alone, ask yourself these questions. Write down your answers.

131

1. What is the purpose of my emotion?

2. What am I telling myself?

3. What can I tell myself instead?

Practice your new self-talk so it will be available to you the next time.

You can also apply this method to your adult relationships. Think about times when you've been annoyed, angry, or hurt. What was the purpose of your emotions? What were you telling yourself? How can you change your thinking?

Chapter 5
Nurturing Emotional and Social Development

What You Will Learn

- Emotions express a child's beliefs and goals.

- Understanding emotional and social development can help you deal with behavior challenges.

- The development of social interest is a major goal in early childhood.

Emotional and Cognitive Milestones

In order to help children grow to be confident and capable people, we need to understand how they relate to their feelings. For a child, learning to connect feelings with thinking is a developmental process that takes place over time. Gaining the ability to handle emotions plays an important part in the child's growing sense of self-esteem. It increases the ability to find positive ways of belonging in the world.

In our work with children, it is important to be aware of and sensitive to the children's emotions. This isn't always easy. Sometimes adults feel that children's emotions are barriers to development. If a child cries easily, adults tend to cringe and hope he will "outgrow it." If a child angers quickly and takes it out physically on others, we hope she won't always be that aggressive. But waiting and hoping are not always helpful. As early childhood teachers, it's our job to help children gain the emotional self-direction they need for successful social development. The first step is understanding the part that emotions play in children's lives.

Children interact with the world emotionally from the beginning of their lives—long before they learn to talk or think logically. Emotions are a basic form of energy that come from the immediate feeling states of hurt, pleasure, discomfort—the things babies experience as soon as they are born.

Each child develops emotionally and socially in her own pace and style—with starts, stops, and retreats along the way. Sometimes emotions are involved in children's misbehavior. This kind of behavior is often a sign that the children are exploring ways to find their place. It's all part of the learning process each child experiences—like learning to walk or talk.

Understanding the early emotional and social development of children helps teachers know how to plan effective learning activities. It also helps us find ways to give positive support and encouragement to children as they develop.

Stanley Greenspan[1] has identified four stages that children go through in the process of normal emotional and intellectual development. According to Greenspan, emotional and cognitive milestones are equally important in this process.

> **Stages of Emotional and Intellectual Development**
>
> **1.** Engagement
>
> **2.** Two-way communication
>
> **3.** Shared meanings
>
> **4.** Emotional thinking

Engagement. In a baby's first four months, he learns to focus his attention, engage with caring adults, share attention, and fall in love with the world. At four to eight months, the engagement process moves toward alternating expressions between adult and child. For example, the baby initiates, the adult responds, and the baby responds to the adult's response. Smiling, reaching, body language, verbal sounds, and crying are all efforts babies make to engage adults.

> *Six-month-old Javetta is learning to make different sounds. She purses her lips and makes a raspberry sound. Her teacher laughs and repeats the sound back to Javetta. They smile and laugh at each other.*

During this happy time of engagement, we need to be aware of opportunities to initiate and respond to babies' first efforts to share their awareness and feelings. Remember, both our verbal and nonverbal adult responses can communicate to the child, "I hear (or see) you, and I understand your feelings."

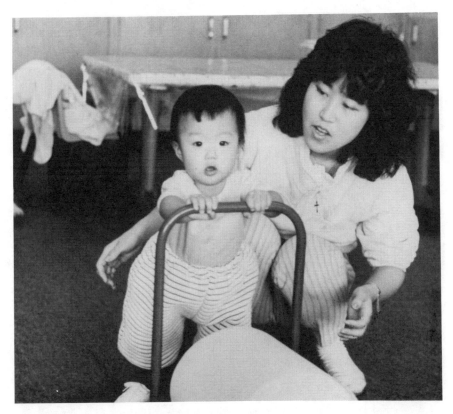

Two-way communication. From six to eighteen months, the child can communicate with the adult through gestures and expressions. Smiles, waves, and reaching are all ways of communicating.

One-year-old Seth enjoys playing peek-a-boo. His teacher holds her hands over her eyes and says, "Peek-a-boo, Seth!" Seth pulls her hands down and laughs at her. Next he holds his blanket over his face. Seth's teacher says, "Where's Seth?" and then pulls down his blanket.

Fifteen-month Kyle drains his cup. He holds it out to his teacher and makes a sound resembling the word "more." His teacher says, "Do you want more, Kyle?" She refills the cup and hands it back to him.

Shared meanings. The next process begins during the toddler period—eighteen to thirty-six months. The child and adults have time to develop communication with its own "code" of meanings. A child may have sounds or words he uses to communicate happiness, fear, or other emotions. Adults may have pet phrases, sounds, or names for the toddler that provoke laughter or smiles from the child.

Two-year-old Amelia encounters a real elephant for the first time on a visit to the zoo. As the animal comes into view, Amelia grabs her teacher's leg and says, "Boom-boom!" The teacher takes Amelia's hand and reassures her. She knows that "boom-boom" is what Amelia says when she is frightened. The toddler learned to say the phrase during a thunderstorm, and is now using it to express her fear in another context.

As a teacher of many children, you may feel challenged by the idea of trying to keep track of all their individual phrases and meanings. Fortunately, there are many widely shared expressions. If you're not sure what meaning a toddler is expressing, try using a tentative response such as, "Are you sad right now?" or, "Could it be you're mad because you spilled the juice?"

A tentative response asks toddlers to make up their own minds and teaches them words for feelings.

Emotional thinking. The fourth stage in the process of emotional and intellectual development starts when children can begin to think consciously about their feelings. At this point, toddlers begin to categorize ideas together with experience—such as "I don't want to play with Mike 'cause he's mean." Children begin to connect ideas with each other and to distinguish reality from fantasy. They also begin to develop problem-solving skills.

> *Five-year-old Cassius wants a turn at the typewriter in the language corner. Two other children are waiting too. Cassius knows about taking turns, but emotionally, he is still anxious he won't get one, and he feels grumpy. Cassius goes to the teacher and says, "Can we make a list of names of people who want a turn to type?" His teacher compliments Cassius by saying, "That's a great idea. With a list, we'll know the right order for people taking turns. After people are done typing, they can cross their names off the list."*

Emotions and Misbehavior

Thinking and emotions are closely tied together. We may not always be aware of it, but we actually *determine* our own emotions on the basis of what we think. Consider how different your emotional response to a defiant child will be depending on whether you think: *"He can't talk to me like that!" —or—"He must be too stressed. It's the end of the day, and he's tired."*

Thinking and emotions also go hand-in-hand in children. But children are not often conscious of the connection—particularly when they are younger.

- A child's best friend is picked up early. The child begins to cry with disappointment.

- You mistakenly hold a picture upside down. The children have never seen this before, and they burst out laughing.

- A child doesn't get something, and begins a temper tantrum of kicking, screaming, and crying.

In each example, the child's thought—*"I want my friend to stay," "That looks silly," "I want my way,"*—has a corresponding and immediate emotion.

As children mature, they begin to connect actions and results. They realize they can use emotional behavior to make things happen. Children explore ways of using their emotions in their relationships. Consider three-year-old Stephanie, for example:

Babies cry to communicate their physical and emotional needs. When they cry, they may be telling us they're hurting, hungry, or tired. They may be sad, angry, frightened, or lonely—or maybe they've simply had too much excitement.

> *Stephanie is physically small for her age. On the playground she often compensates for her size by assertively using a loud voice. But when other children push or shove, she immediately starts to cry, and the aide comes running.*
>
> *At snacktime, Stephanie takes a graham cracker from a plate next to hers. When the other girl begins to protest, the teacher says, "Stephanie, you know taking Caitlyn's cookie is not very nice." Stephanie begins to cry. The teacher says, "I know you feel sad. That's okay. But it's not okay to take any more cookies from Caitlyn."*
>
> *At home after dinner, Stephanie asks for dessert but is told there is no dessert tonight. She begins to cry. To stop the crying, her mom goes to the cupboard in search of something Stephanie can have for dessert.*

These are three situations, three crying incidents, and three different purposes for the same emotional device—tears. Stephanie has discovered that "water power" is an effective means to get her way.

Emotions are not accidental—like Stephanie's tears, they can be used to make things happen. In Stephanie's case, understanding the *goal* of her emotions can help us understand her behavior. As children get older, it is often useful to look for emotions that are being used as tools for achieving misbehavior goals. (See Chapter 1 for more information on misbehavior goals in older children.)

Some children learn early the effectiveness of "water power."

Skills for Dealing with Emotions and Misbehavior

Children's emotional development is greatly helped by a supportive environment in which adults are understanding and encouraging. As teachers, we can take specific steps to help children develop healthy emotional expression. There are also skills we can use to deal with emotions when they give rise to misbehavior.

Use reflective listening to help children recognize and express their feelings. *"You seem unhappy." "You look confused."*

Be encouraging. Encouragement is a major method for dealing with emotional misbehavior. Since emotional misbehavior is a reflection of a child's <u>dis</u>couragement, <u>en</u>couragement is an effective response.

Avoid labels. Adult responses to children's words or actions may be judgmental. These judgments, even if positive, can have a discouraging effect. Whenever possible, avoid using labels such as *good, bad,* or *stubborn*. Even "good" labels can be discouraging, because they place the child in a dependent position where the child feels evaluated. See Chapter 2 for a complete discussion of encouragement.

Respect each child's uniqueness. This helps build self-esteem. It also helps personalize the adult-child relationship. *"You like to sing while you play with your blocks."*

Sadness can be a cry for help. We must decide what the child is telling us with the sadness.

139

Be aware of children's feelings. Indicate clearly that you recognize and understand them. *"I hear the siren, too. It sounds scary."*

Help children see that it's possible to have confusing or contradictory feelings—to love and be angry with someone at the same time. *"Sometimes you like to play with Jameel, but you get angry when he takes your toys."*

Balance your understanding with appropriate limits. *"I see you're angry because Glenda broke Dolly's arm. But people aren't for hitting. Come play over here till you're not so angry."*

Be aware of the importance of security objects. One way infants and small children cope with their emotions is by depending on objects such as their thumb or a special blanket for self-comfort.

As children move from babyhood to toddler and preschool age, they are continually learning about emotions. During the early years we can help children by understanding their emotions. As they grow, they can learn how to cope with their own emotions with our help and modeling.

Ten-month-old Evette is crying and kicking on the changing table. Her teacher says calmly, "I know you don't like being changed. We'll be quick. I'll sing to you while I change you." She sings to help Evette through the hard time.

Emotional Challenges

Many challenges can come up as teachers and children deal with emotions. We can't examine them all, but we will consider some situations that often occur in early childhood settings.

Responding to Emotional Challenges

Three guidelines are useful in assessing what to do with any emotional challenge:

- What is the purpose of this behavior?

- Is any response (attention) appropriate, or should I ignore this emotion?

- This child is discouraged. How can I encourage him now, and once more later today?

Crying

An infant's cry is his first verbal means of communication. Babies cry to communicate their physical and emotional needs. When they cry, they may be telling us they're hurting, hungry, or tired. They may be sad, angry, frightened, or lonely—or maybe they've simply had too much excitement.

> *Six-month-old Mickey had frequent ear infections. He had trouble sleeping and often woke crying if he rolled over in his sleep. His teacher learned to quiet him by rocking him and rubbing his back. After Mickey's ear infections cleared up, he still had trouble quieting down for a nap. His teacher would rock him and rub his back, but Mickey would still cry whenever he was put down in his crib. Gradually his teacher ended the pattern of first rocking Mickey and then rubbing his back after she laid him down. It took a week before Mickey had settled back into regular naps, but his teacher knew Mickey needed to learn ways to comfort himself and relax.*

Toddlers and preschoolers communicate by crying, too. Because young children have difficulty putting their feelings into words, they often express some feelings by crying. It seems a natural reaction to pick up and reassure a crying child with a hug and a few kind words. Sometimes this is the wise thing to do. But we need to be aware that tears can become powerful emotional tools, too. Children learn that emotional displays—crying, kicking, screaming—can be used to get attention or to engage in a power struggle.

We have to walk a fine line between sensitivity for a single child and awareness of the needs of the entire group.

> *Four-year-old Jean likes to talk with you. He's proud of his new shoes and wants to tell you all about them. After you listen a while, you move on, but he begins to cling to your knee. You gently remove him without saying anything, but he begins to cry softly. When you walk away, he begins to cry loudly.*

Based on what you believe to be the purpose of crying behavior, you can choose a possible response:

- Ignore the crying, because it is for attention.

- Respond with a reflection such as, "You seem upset that I have to go."

- Redirect the child with a request for assistance or some other distraction.

> *Three-year-old Bjorn loves the rocking chair in the book area. The rocking chair provides him with a safe place to survey the room and the other children. One day Bjorn comes in and finds another child rocking in the chair. Bjorn bursts into tears and sobs, "My chair!" The teacher points out that the chair is for the whole class to use, but Bjorn starts crying louder.*

Temper tantrums need an audience.

The teacher might choose to ignore the crying, but she realizes that Bjorn needs a quiet place when he first arrives in the morning. She says, "Bjorn, why don't you sit on my lap for a minute and watch the other children? You can rock in the chair later."

Crying isn't always misbehavior. A careful look at the situation and our own feelings and responses will help us avoid children's use of crying to achieve negative goals.

Sadness

Sadness can be a cry for help. We must decide what the child is telling us with the sadness. It may be a direct response to the loss of a pet, friend, or other major disappointment. Helping the child talk about this and listening to feelings are ways we can help.

Older toddlers and preschoolers sometimes use sadness to gain attention.

> *Four-year-old Carrie is riding the tricycle. Her teacher says her turn is over. Carrie bursts into tears. Her teacher says, "I can tell you're sad but you've had a long turn and it's Rhonda's turn to ride the tricycle now." If Carrie continues crying, the teacher might direct her to a quiet area of the playground and tell her, "When you're done crying, come tell me what you're going to do next."*

As with all attention seeking, we must find ways to give attention at times when the child is not demanding it.

Sadness may also be a method a child has learned in order to manage her other feelings. Feelings of loneliness, inadequacy, anger, or depression may appear on the surface as sadness. It is important to determine the underlying meaning and purpose of a child's sadness. When dealing with a child who is sad:

- Help the child talk about his feelings.

- Treat the feelings seriously—do not trivialize them. Treat the child's concerns with respect.

- If a child is sad for an extended period of time, let a parent know what you have observed. Parents may want to seek the advice of a pediatrician or professional counselor.

> *Five-year-old Delores seems sad and low on energy many days. When her teacher asks her if she wants to try an activity, Delores often says she's too tired. One day, Delores' teacher sits beside her and says, "Delores, I've noticed that you often look sad. Can you tell me what's bothering you?" Tears well up in Delores' eyes and then she whispers, "My mom and dad had a big fight. Dad left. I don't know where he is." Delores' teacher hugs her and says, "I'm really glad you told me. It's scary when parents fight. I'll talk to your mom and see if she can tell you about your dad."*

Fear and Anxiety

Children's fears and anxieties tell us about their emotional concerns. We may see these concerns as children react warily or fearfully in situations.

> *Four-year-old Maggie's first day at the center begins with her mother dragging her into the room. Maggie shouts "NO NO NO! I'm not going away!" at the top of her lungs.*

The best guideline for handling fears and anxieties is to be sensitive and supportive to the child. This seems to be common sense, but how is it practical with a large group of children? If you spend all your time with one fearful child, won't the others be neglected? Or worse—won't this show the others the best way to get some of your time is to be fearful?

> *Three-year-old Harry screams when he sees a housefly in the room. His teacher reassures him that the fly won't hurt him, but Harry continues yelling and runs away. When the teacher mentions the incident to Harry's mom, she explains that Harry was recently stung by a bee.*

Harry's teacher now has a clearer picture of Harry's underlying problem. She can help defuse Harry's fears by talking about insects with all the children.

We have to walk a fine line between sensitivity for a single child and awareness of the needs of the entire group. We'll talk about working with the group later, but first let's focus on T. Berry Brazelton's[2] suggestions for handling children's fears.

143

You and Your Relationships
As adults, we all carry around in us the results of our early emotional and social development process. If you are experiencing emotional or social stress with a coworker or another adult, think about it by looking for clues in these areas, just as you do for children. What are the unspoken goals of the difficult feelings and behaviors? If you were a teacher dealing with children who had similar problems, how might you try to help?

Communicate "It's okay to be afraid." If you respond to a fearful child in a way that calmly accepts his fear, your listening or brief reflection of the situation may be enough. *"I know you're scared when the dog barks. You're doing fine."* Placating responses such as "Don't worry," or "There's nothing to be afraid of," may be true—for you. The child has just indicated she is worried and afraid! Communicating with the child in a matter-of-fact voice helps in this situation.

When the fire bell rings for the fire drill, several of the toddlers scream and cover their ears. The teacher says, "I know it's loud, but we need to practice leaving the school quickly. We're practicing what we would do if there were a real fire." Because the teacher knows that two-and-a-half-year-old Michelle is particularly afraid of the fire bell noise, she made sure she knew the time of the drill beforehand, so she could be standing near Michelle to reassure her when the bell sounded.

Understand the reasons for the fears. What might be the goal of a child's fearfulness? His fears may either allow him to control a situation, or to withdraw and not take part. Fear can sometimes be used by a preschooler to get attention or power. It can also be the trigger for aggressive behavior. Reassure the child that there are more positive ways to be assertive, such as learning how to express feelings directly.

Five-year-old LaMar and three-year-old Becky are playing together, but LaMar takes all the toys. Becky begins to whimper and an adult comes over to say, "You want to play with LaMar. Why don't you ask him to share, or play over here with Jessie?"

Stick to rules and keep ordinarily acceptable boundaries. It is important to know the purpose of a child's fear or anxiety when you're deciding which activities to ask the child to do. For instance, a child may act fearful of the playground, but you would still keep the rule that everyone goes outside when it's playtime. In another situation, a child might not want to get into the wading pool. You would not force the child to get into the water, although you might encourage him to play *near* the water.

Two-and-a-half-year-old Miguel is terrified of anyone dressed up in a costume. Today a clown is visiting the school to show children how she puts on her clown makeup and costume. Miguel's teacher decides it's important for him to see this. She explains to Miguel that he must stay in the room with the clown, but it's fine if he wants to sit in the back of the room in the assistant teacher's lap. Miguel does so, protesting, and then watches in fascination as the clown applies her makeup.

Making up stories and exaggerating are typical behavior, especially in older preschoolers.

This guideline suggests a need to be sensitive to the children, but also realize the underlying purpose of their concerns.

Help children become aware of outlets for feelings. We can use puppets, stories, or other activities which actively teach children about feelings.

With older children, the key to good transitions is letting them know what is going to happen and what you expect of them. Remember, too, to use your sense of humor.

Helping Children and Parents Handle Separation Anxiety

For many children, preschool is their first extended experience with separation from their parents. Separation fears are normal, and we can expect outbursts from children from time to time. As teachers, we want to communicate respect to children while we help them overcome their fears.

To lessen the effects of separation anxiety:

- Instruct parents (through handouts or prior meetings) to leave without lingering, but always to tell the child that they will be back.

- In the morning, greet the child by name and talk to him in a calm, friendly manner. Reflect the child's concern fully and respectfully: *"I see you're sad that your dad is leaving. He'll be back later."*

- Hold out your hand, or offer the child a lap to sit in while he regains his emotional balance. Some children may be ready to shift focus after just a few minutes. Others may need a period of quiet time to themselves. Respect the child's personal style. Child and parent will both be helped if you handle the situation with an attitude of calm, confidence, and gentle firmness.

- As soon as possible, guide the child in the direction of friends, toys, or favorite activities.

- You may want to suggest the parent leave a belonging (such as a scarf) with the child—mentioning that it will be retrieved when the parent comes back to pick up the child. If anxiety returns during the day, it may reassure the child to see the object or carry it around for awhile.

- In group activities, focus on the idea that it's okay to feel afraid when a parent leaves in the morning. Assure children that everyone has these feelings sometimes, but they do pass.

Parents often experience separation anxieties, too. Parents don't like to cause their children distress. They may feel fearful, guilty, regretful, or embarrassed about leaving their child in child care. Children sense their parent's attitudes—which may heighten the separation anxiety for both. So it is important for you to help parents handle their anxious feelings, too.

Temper Tantrums

Temper tantrums need an audience. In a preschool center there is always an audience! The tantrum is one of a child's most upsetting behaviors. As teachers in the situation, we too may feel angry, embarrassed, or out of control.

There are two kinds of tantrums. Each kind calls for a specific approach. The first step is to determine which kind of tantrum the child is using.

Type 1: The "frustration" tantrum. This tantrum occurs when things are simply not going the child's way. A tower of blocks so carefully constructed is accidentally knocked over. The child knew how to tie his shoes yesterday, but today the laces seem to be made of spaghetti! A sense of failure may explode into a tantrum. *If possible,* let the child cry out this kind of tantrum. When the child is through, you can hold or comfort him: "It's hard when accidents happen." "It's really sad when your shoes just don't tie."

Trying to help right at the point of failure or anger may not work, because the child is too caught up in his own feelings. You probably remember times when you were so angry that you didn't want to listen to soothing words from anyone. Adults sometimes need to let off steam before they can begin to hear others again. The same thing is true of children.

If we let the child express these strong feelings, won't the other children get the message that tantrums are all right? Children are keen observers. If the teacher is not alarmed, upset, or impressed by such a display of emotions, it is less likely the children will be. Watching your reactions, they will come to understand that sometimes these out-of-control feelings can happen. But they will also learn there are better ways of handling anger. These positive behaviors should be encouraged and noticed as the children learn them.

Type 2: The "weapon" tantrum. At other times, a child may throw a tantrum to gain power, or express revenge. His goal may be to get you to give in to a demand, or to get even for a perceived injustice. Specific guidelines for dealing with "weapon tantrums" are:

- Whenever possible, ignore the behavior.

- If possible, not only ignore the behavior but immediately pay attention to someone else who is behaving well.

- If the temper tantrum continues, tell the child a time-out may occur if he doesn't calm down: "If you keep on screaming, you'll need to go to the Calm-Down Place for awhile."

- Place the child in the Calm-Down Place. Either do it without words, or just make a brief comment that she will have a chance to come back into the group when she has settled down.

Three-year-old Fiona is used to getting her own way at home. At the learning center, Fiona often has to negotiate to get her way. Today the grocery store is set up and Fiona wants to run the cash register. She says, "I want it." Dana pulls the register back and says, "I had it first." Fiona throws herself on the floor and begins screaming and kicking. Fiona's teacher intervenes and says, "Fiona, Dana has the cash register now. You can be a customer or you can stock the shelves with cans and boxes."

If Fiona calms down and agrees, the teacher might suggest that Fiona could have a turn with the cash register when Dana is done. However, if Fiona continues screaming and grabbing at the cash register, the teacher might choose to remove her from the dramatic play area.

The most effective way to deal with tantrums is to prevent them from happening in the first place. While this isn't always possible, we can watch for times when we may set up tantrum behavior by letting a situation go on too long or not attending to a child's level of stress or fatigue. When this happens, distraction may work as a way of handling the situation if the tantrum is mild, but Type 2 tantrum behavior might be first ignored, and then the child can be removed from the group.

Stress and Physical Symptoms
All young children experience stress in their lives. Some children may react to stress with physical symptoms such as headaches, stomachaches, or nervous tics. We cannot control all of the sources of stress, but we can examine our routines to see if we are adding to the stresses on children. Some ways to reduce stress are:

- Reduce competitiveness, especially in games. One winner usually means many losers.

- Encourage any efforts and signs of progress.

- Create an atmosphere in which the children feel unconditionally accepted.

- Help a child be realistic about expectations and results.

- Give children opportunities to express cooperation.

- Teach relaxation skills.

- Set aside times for calming down. For example, when coming back from the playground, have the group do slow swinging or stretching to help calm down.

It helps children when we let them know we understand when they are uncomfortable. If you believe a child's symptom is stress-related, the most helpful thing to do may be to find ways to help the child express or reduce the stress.

Symptoms which continue over time need to be called to the attention of the parents. It may be helpful to work cooperatively with parents on ways to reduce stress on the child both at home and at the center. Not all physical symptoms are caused by stress. Aches and pains that are sharp, get worse and more frequent, and are accompanied by other symptoms such as vomiting or vision difficulties need to be treated as medical problems. See Chapter 6 for more information on ways to work with parents, including conferences.

Understanding Children's Social Development

Social development occurs in children at the same time their emotional development is taking place. As children mature, they build relationships with peers and adults. In this section, we will examine ways to help children build their social relationship skills.

A major factor in children's social development is their need for independence. When a two year-old pushes aside your offer of help with a determined "I do it!", he is expressing this desire. The drive toward independence is very strong, but it is not the child's only goal. A few minutes later, the same child may come running for a hug and emotional support. A child's rapidly changing needs and feelings make developing social relationships a challenge for everyone—especially other children, who are dealing with feelings of their own.

Working with Parents
If a child is a repetitive biter, you can bring in the parents to talk about the issue—they may be having the same problem at home. Talk with them about the child's situation at home. Is there a new baby, for instance? Deciding on a cooperative, consistent approach to handling aggression in both locations is likely to decrease the number of biting incidents overall. It will also help the child learn new behavior patterns for handling his feelings.

Sociability begins to develop early.

Stages of Social Development

Babies reach out and coo to familiar adults and children. They are developing trust relationships with parents and other caregivers. They may begin to resist separations from familiar adults at around eight to ten months.

Between twelve and twenty-four months, children begin to be interested in developing relationships with peers, first by watching or imitating their play, then as a companion playing side-by-side with them.

Three-year-olds are learning to take turns and share, even though they may still want to play alone.

Four-year-olds are better able to cooperate, play together, and participate in group activities. This is the beginning of close friendships and "best friends." Four-year-olds' active imaginations often create imaginary friends and pets.

Five-year-olds enjoy relationships. Fives have a greater capacity for cooperation and more social interest. They are particularly attentive to younger children.

Encouraging Social Interest

It is important to help children develop the ability and willingness to cooperate with one another, as well as with adults. We call this the ability to display social interest. The child who cares about others and cooperates with them is on the right track. How can we help children develop these attitudes?

Encourage children to help at an early age.

- "Who would like to help water the bean plants?"

- "Would you like to give this toilet paper tube to the gerbil?"

- "Please help me pass out napkins and cups. Thanks!"

Let children take care of their own mistakes. Spills and breaks are normal events, and it is reasonable to ask the children to help clean up.

- "Oops! The juice spilled. Please go get a sponge and wipe it up."

- "I'm sorry your picture tore. Do you want some tape to fix it?"

Don't expect perfection. Do recognize efforts and progress.

For younger children, clear expectations and reliable routines are helpful in coping with activity changes.

> *In the four-year-old room, Mark and Sally played with puzzles together for ten minutes. Now they are beginning to squabble. The teacher says to them, "You played so nicely together today. Let's put the puzzle away and get ready for a snack."*

Don't change a child's first results.

> *Four-year-old Marbella is learning to button her coat. After fumbling for a while, she gets the coat buttoned, but the buttons are crooked. Marbella's teacher compliments her on her efforts by saying, "Look at you, Marbella! You buttoned your own coat."*

Create opportunities for playing together.

> *The five-year-olds have invited the three-year-olds to a special holiday celebration. They sing some songs for the three-year-olds and then sit with them at the snack table to share some special cookies they've decorated.*

Notice and encourage children's attempts to play cooperatively.

Two-year-old Trevor crawls into the wagon. His friend Shiro tries to push him, but the wagon is too heavy and it won't budge. The teacher says, "Shiro, I can see you were trying to give Trevor a ride. That wagon is really heavy."

Social Development Challenges

Behavior challenges that come with social development involve many factors. By this point in your study, you are already familiar with:

- goal-directed behavior in children.

- developmentally appropriate behavior.

- ways of encouraging and listening to children.

- how to create a consistent discipline system.

Using these skills regularly will give you the most effective approach to dealing with social development behavior problems.

Honesty

When you are faced with a specific situation involving honesty, ask yourself—is the issue here dishonesty or exaggeration? Making up stories and exaggerating are typical behavior, especially in older preschoolers. Children sometimes use dishonesty to gain attention or to avoid a consequence of their behavior. When possible, don't overreact or be impressed by children's dishonest statements. Sometimes, you can even ignore them.

Five-year-old Rodney twirls around and accidentally knocks a plant off the science table. When the teacher hears the crash, he asks, "What happened?" Rodney quickly replies, "I didn't do it!" and runs off. Rodney's teacher follows him and says, "Rodney, I'm not mad at you for knocking the plant down—accidents happen. But you need to help me clean up the dirt."

Four-year-old Jaleesa's mother recently lost her job, and finances are tight. One day Jaleesa comes to school and announces, "We're going to Disney World!" Jaleesa's teacher knows this isn't true, but she understands Jaleesa's wishes, so she says, "I bet you wish you could go to Disney World. It would be lots of fun."

Sharing

When children are not sharing, they may be tired, angry, or simply not ready to share. Everyone would like children to share, but when it does not happen, ask yourself, "Is it realistic to expect sharing at this time? Should one child be removed from the situation, or can they share?"

The preschool teacher has just put two new calculators in the pretend store. A group of children swarms around her asking for a turn. Since the calculators are a new addition to the room, the teacher realizes everyone will want a turn to try them out. She says, "I'm going to make a list of everyone who wants to try a calculator. Then I'm going to set this kitchen timer and each child will get a five minute turn. When the bell dings your turn is over, and the next person gets a try."

Jealousy

Jealousy is another way of saying "I want . . . !" Jealousy is a feeling that occurs often in the early years. It is a particularly strong emotion for children from the ages of eighteen months to three-and-a-half-years. During that time, a child may be having to share parents' attention with a new baby at home. Often, children may be having their first experience with other children, and facing the challenges of sharing and cooperation at the same time.

We can't totally get rid of jealousy in children, and it's not necessary to do so. Experiencing jealousy helps children face up to the challenges in life, which in turn helps them to mature. We can assist in making the jealousy less intense by helping children to understand their jealous feelings.

- "You're feeling angry now because Miss Ellen needs to help Simon with his lunch."

- "Could you be feeling sad because Abby got to the other side of the playground first?"

Sharing and jealousy go hand-in-hand.

> *Twelve-month-old Sheena has become very attached to her teacher. Whenever another child crawls in the teacher's lap or asks to be held, Sheena starts screaming. Sheena's teacher says, "I know it's hard to share, but everybody needs hugs. I'll hold you soon, Sheena."*

Transition Times

Transition times—when children are moving between activities or locations—are times when behavior problems often occur. This is because it is hard for children to change gears as they shift focus. They need our help to learn how to make transitions smoothly.

Transitions can be difficult for children *and* teachers. It's best not to let them be too abrupt.

154

Activity changes. Transition times require special care and cooperation by staff members. It often helps to have one teacher stay engaged with the children as they finish up an activity, while another staff member sets up the next one.

> *The teacher and her aide have been talking with the toddlers about their coloring projects. Now it is time to get out the rhythm instruments and clear an area for group music play. The teacher and aide begin moving aside tables and chairs at the other end of the room. Soon several of the children come running over, scattering papers and crayons. A squabble breaks out and the happy atmosphere begins to deteriorate.*
>
> *The teacher moves back to the group and says, "It's going to be time to finish up these art projects in a minute or two. If you're ready to stop drawing now, let's begin putting things away. Then we'll read a story while Miss Jeanette sets up the music game we're going to play next."*

It's not always possible to divide up duties between teachers this way. It is also valuable for children to learn they can handle transition times without a teacher's direct involvement. The key is to let the children know what is happening and what they need to do to cooperate.

> *The children in the four-year-old room have been playing in the housekeeping area. The next activity involves working with floor mats and a parachute. The teacher does not have a staff member available to help her set up and make the transition. So she goes to the group and says, "Pretty soon we are going to be doing some fun stuff with a parachute, and I need to get it ready. You guys finish up playing here, and be patient while I'm busy, okay? When you're ready, start putting the toys away carefully. I'll be back to help you finish before we play the parachute game."*

Children can get distracted if a staff member is setting up a new activity while they are involved in free play. It is helpful to keep children busy with a specific group task during this "change of gears" time. Letting the children know they need to be ready for a change in a few minutes and that you want them to be patient while you prepare the next activity will help the transition go more smoothly.

Sandra Crosser[3] suggests that signals can be useful in cueing transition times. For instance, a designated tune played on the piano can signal cleanup time. A bell, sign, hand signal, or flick of the lights can signal time to gather for a story. Signals should be low key so as not to startle or frighten the children.

Crosser also suggests that finger plays, rhymes, and action songs can be very useful methods of intriguing children who have become inattentive or who need to be brought together into a group for a new activity. Children love the fun and challenge of finger plays. When the finger play has been completed, children are refocused and ready to listen. Short action songs can be used in the same manner. Both finger plays and action songs are available in source books from libraries or educational supply houses.

Location changes. Transition times often involve moving groups of children from one location to another. With older children, the key to good transitions is letting them know what is going to happen and what you expect of them. Remember, too, to use your sense of humor.

The four- and five-year-olds are going on a walking trip that will end up at a local gymnasium where they will practice running and jumping skills. The teacher calls the children together and tells them where they are going, how they will get there, and what they are to do when they arrive.

The teacher says to the children, "I am going to divide you into 'sandwiches' with four people each. You decide who will be the pieces of bread and what will be in between—one person can be peanut butter and somebody else can be jelly." The teacher designates the groups. She says, "I want each sandwich to stay together with the bread pieces on the outside as we walk to the gym. As we walk, I'll ask the leaders to go just as far as I say, and then stop. Once everybody is together, we'll go to the next stopping place. Okay? Great. Now . . . when we get to the gym I'll go in first. When you get inside, find the wide yellow line that goes around the floor and run all the way around it two times. Everybody got that? Okay—here we go!" *

For younger children, clear expectations and reliable routines are helpful in coping with activity changes.

---

* Ideas in this example come from Sandra Crosser, "Managing the Early Childhood Classroom." Young Children, January 1992.

> *The children in the preschool room know that every day, snacks follow storytime. When the teacher finishes the story, each child puts away the carpet square he's been sitting on and goes to the sink to wash his hands. The teacher doesn't even need to remind the children of the sequence, because they've done it so often.*

Naptime. Another helpful suggestion for transitions with younger children is to let each child take one book or toy with her to her cot at naptime. A few minutes of quiet individual play can help children wind down.

End of the Day

The end of the day can be another stressful time for children. Children whose parents arrive later than others may begin to feel worried about being left behind. Fatigue can make anxiety harder for everyone to handle. Teachers can do several things to help:

- Reflect the child's feelings clearly and kindly: "You want to go home like Billy did."

- Reassure children that their parents will arrive: "You're looking forward to seeing your mommy. She'll be here pretty soon."

- Involve the children in an activity such as listening to a story tape on the cassette recorder, so the time will pass quickly.

Aggression—Biting, Hitting, Pushing

Aggressive behavior can be lessened by:

- Reflective listening

- Giving choices

- Removing the child when the behavior is inappropriate

It isn't realistic to expect that children will never be aggressive. However, we can understand that this behavior is purposeful.

> *Five-year-old Valerie and four-year-old Amado have been bickering all morning. Valerie pushes Amado off the swing and climbs on herself. Amado responds by kicking Valerie. In a minute, they are rolling in the grass, punching and calling each other names. When the teacher arrives, he separates them and says, "You're having trouble getting along. You'll need to play on separate parts of the playground away from each other."*

Biting. Biting can be a problem, especially with younger children. When it happens, it is frightening to other children and upsetting to adults. Biting often occurs during transition times because these are the hardest times of the day for children. Biting is a problem that requires the skill of structuring by staff members. If you have a child who bites frequently, look at the situations in which he bites. What is typically going on at those times? The key to the problem is keeping him out of those situations, or structuring them in ways that will help the child modify his behavior.

> *Two-and-a-half-year-old Turrell frequently has trouble with biting when he comes in from outside play, which he loves, and settles down for a nap, which he does not like to do. The other children often feel afraid of Turrell, and sometimes they don't want to play with him or nap next to him. This has a bad effect on Turrell's self-esteem, which increases his anti-social biting behavior.*
>
> *The teacher wants to help Turrell move beyond this cycle of misbehavior. At the end of outside time, she hands him a ball or some other toy to carry inside each day. This helps give Turrell focus and purpose on his way inside. It keeps his hands busy, and gives him extra adult attention at a time when he needs encouragement.*
>
> *At naptime, the teacher has an aide help Turrell finish with his cleanup after snacks. She sits with him quietly for a few minutes (in her lap, if he feels like it) while the other children get settled for rest. When the group is quietly playing with toys on their cots, the aide helps Turrell settle on his cot and stays near for awhile, until it is clear that the children are beginning to relax and rest.*

An older child who bites may need to learn to use words to express feelings in stressful situations. Talk to the child directly about the issue, saying that you know she bites when she feels angry or worried. Ask her to remember how she felt at the time of a recent biting incident. Discuss her feelings, and suggest other ways of handling them. Let the child know you will be there to help her handle situations in other ways if it would help. Tell her it's okay to feel angry, but emphasize clearly that biting is not okay. If she bites again, she will have decided to go to the Calm-Down Place.

If a time-out is needed, use the opportunity to review with the child the feelings that led to the biting. Help her think again about different ways to handle her feelings. If the biting persists, the child may be using this behavior to attain a goal of attention or power. Treat further biting like "weapon" tantrum behavior, removing the biter firmly and immediately from the group with little comment or attention.

Toileting. Coordination with the parents about toilet training is important, because it helps children when adult expectations are consistent. Occasionally sharing positive comments with the parents and the child about success at home or at the center is a way of giving attention that can encourage a child in his toilet training efforts.

When it comes to toilet training, it is crucial to respect a child's developmental level. Children aren't usually physically able to control bowel and bladder functions until the age of two or later.[4] This means toilet training may be accomplished sometime between the ages of two and three. Be alert to each child's individual readiness. It's important not to pressure children through any of the stages of toilet training.

Treat temporary setbacks in toilet training as unfortunate happenings, not big mistakes.

> *Two-year-old Jordan watches other children use the bathroom at nursery school, and he is beginning to show interest in sitting on a potty chair. His teacher removes his diaper and says, "Jordan, your diaper is dry. Why don't you try going in the potty?" She sits Jordan on the chair for a minute. When he starts to squirm, she lets him get up, puts on a new diaper, and says, "Tell me when your diaper is wet. Later we'll try the potty chair again." Jordan's teacher is encouraging him without turning toileting into a power struggle.*

Most children will be toilet trained by their third birthday. It usually takes boys longer to achieve control than girls. Treat temporary setbacks as unfortunate happenings, not big mistakes. Help the child get clean and dry, and show sensitivity and interest: "You must be uncomfortable. Would you like some dry pants?"

Family problems. Family problems are part of the child's life that come with him into your facility. Death, divorce, arguments, and other events can and do invade the space inside your room. You can't solve these problems, but there are things you can do to help. If a child exhibits increased destructive talk or negative behaviors, you might:

- Recognize the behaviors are a way to gain extra attention. How can you pay positive attention to the child?

- Take care not to overreact when a child occasionally talks about doing damage to himself or others. He may just be venting his anger or making a momentary bid for attention. Repetition of such statements, over a few days or weeks, would be cause for concern. But a child's statement "I'm gonna kill you!" is not, by itself, cause for a psychiatric evaluation.

- Concentrate on finding positive aspects of the child's behavior, in order to build self-esteem.

- Get the child involved with other children who are feeling more positive.

Children Who Arrive Mid-Year
Children come and go in our settings, and we make efforts to help each belong and become part of our groups. Some methods for helping a new child feel welcome include:

- Taking an instant camera picture of the child and putting it on the board with the child's name beneath it.

- Giving the child attention by having a "welcoming interview," asking the child to share information with the group about favorite colors, animals, foods, and family.

- Assigning a "best buddy" for a day.

Children are social beings. As teachers, we need to develop group experiences that help all the children feel a sense of secure belonging.

Notes

1. Stanley Greenspan, *Floor Time* (New York: Scholastic, 1990). This video presentation gives further information on the four stages.

   Stanley Greenspan and Nancy Thorndike Greenspan, *First Feelings* (New York: Viking Penguin, 1985).

2. T. Berry Brazelton, *To Listen to a Child: Understanding the Normal Problems of Growing Up* (Reading, MA: Addison-Wesley, 1984).

3. Sandra Crosser, "Managing the Early Childhood Classroom" *Young Children*, January 1992.

4. Brazelton, p. 162.

Problem Situations

Infant. Fourteen-month-old Tiffany is in an infant-toddler program. Every afternoon Mr. Green, the janitor, vacuums the hall. Tiffany is afraid of the noisy vacuum cleaner as it roars by. She runs shrieking to her teacher. Several of the other children in the group begin crying and screaming too.

1. What are some things Tiffany's teacher can do to help Tiffany?

2. What can the teacher do to calm the other children down?

Toddler. Two-and-a-half-year-old Rebecca is being noisy and disruptive at story time. Her teacher, Miss Kay, asks her to quiet down. Rebecca screams "No!" and sticks out her tongue at the teacher. When Miss Kay ignores this response, Rebecca again starts being noisy and disruptive, and no one can hear the story.

1. What might be the goal of Rebecca's disruptive behavior?

2. What are some things Miss Kay might do to deal with this challenge?

Preschooler. The teacher, Mrs. Lambert, has asked the children to put away the sand toys and be patient with her while she gets the paints ready for art time. Four year old Jamal throws down the shovel he has been digging with and runs after Mrs. Lambert. He tags close beside her, asking questions and demanding help with his sleeves while she is trying to set up the paint containers at the easels.

1. What is Jamal's goal?

2. How could Mrs. Lambert respond to Jamal's behavior in an encouraging way?

Applying Your Skills

Practice applying previously learned skills to emotional and social challenges. For example, you may decide to begin with just one or two child-ren, and focus on temper tantrum behavior or helping a child handle transition anxiety.

Things to Consider

While the skills we present have been found to be effective in most cases, you will want to determine a skill's effectiveness in your situation.

- Examine the child's environment, activities and scheduling factors that may be contributing to the problem.

- Examine any personal liabilities on your part, such as being easy to anger, talking too much, being demanding, having to be in control, trying to be perfect, wanting to please.

- Assess your personal resources for solving this problem. These are qualities or strengths such as a sense of humor, adeptness at problem solving, patience, or being perceptive.

Follow-Up

Your leader will provide time to discuss your results with the group at your next meeting. If your group does not meet again, plan a time to evaluate your efforts with others in your center who have taken the *TLC* class. If the results of the assignment are unsatisfactory, decide how you can modify your approach in the future.

Record Keeping (Optional)

You may find it helpful to log your observations and actions. The following format can be used for your log.

Daily Log   Child's Name: _____

	Child's Behavior	My Action	Results
Monday			
Tuesday			
Wednesday			
Thursday			
Friday			

1. Emotions express a child's desires and intentions. They reflect the child's beliefs and goals.

2. Giving an immediate negative response to a child's emotional display may actually reinforce the emotional problem. Instead, listen—and let the child know clearly that you hear the feeling. This may help the child think about new ways of handling emotions.

3. If you become angry, insistent, or demanding, children will learn more from what you do than what you say.

4. Limits are important in helping the child develop respect and trust. When children observe guidelines set out by adults, they learn self-acceptance and a willingness to work with other people.

5. Children's fears are often a call for help. Listen closely to determine the purpose of the fear and help the child find a more effective way to cope. By helping the child meet the challenge, you help the child develop courage.

6. Separation anxiety is a common experience. You can listen to the child's feelings, accept them, and firmly and kindly help him find ways to make the transition to other activities.

7. Each child develops socially at his or her own rate. You can help foster social growth and prevent disruptive behavior by being aware of each child's individual characteristics, including beliefs, feelings, and level of development.

8. Preschool children learn cooperation and choices from natural and logical consequences. Attempts to punish and control stimulate resistance and fear.

9. Social interest includes cooperation, listening, and appropriate expression of feelings. It is a measure of mental health and social maturity.

10. A basic technique for fostering social interest is to encourage and recognize cooperative behavior. It is more important to reinforce behavior you want to encourage than to comment on behavior you don't want repeated.

The Courage to Be Imperfect*

Emotional distress often comes from thinking patterns and belief systems. Emotions are closely tied to thinking. We can help ourselves by using our thoughts to affect our emotions in positive ways.

"I must be perfect" or "I can't make a mistake" are thoughts which can lead to stress, burnout, and emotional distress. If you hold these beliefs, you may tend to see negative events as catastrophic and out of proportion.

Regardless of how you usually approach things, examine these statements as helpful ways to think about the things you do each day:

- I have the courage to be imperfect, to risk new behaviors, and to try new ideas.

- Mistakes are learning opportunities.

Food for thought:

- In what ways is it all right to be imperfect today?

- What mistakes did you make today that will help you learn?

---

* The concept of "The Courage to Be Imperfect" was originally developed by Dr. Rudolph Dreikurs.

Chapter 6
Working in Partnership with Parents

What You Will Learn

- Regular communication between home and school is important.

- Adults base their actions on priorities and beliefs.

- It is important to develop common goals and expectations with parents.

- Parents need to hear positives about children, even when there are problems.

Supporting Children's First Steps into the World

As we work with young children, we share an important responsibility with parents and other other primary caregivers. The children move between two worlds—one at home, and the other at the early childhood center.

Douglas Powell[1] believes there are three underlying assumptions that point to the importance of a strong relationship between families and early childhood programs. These assumptions are:

1. Teachers need to be aware that differences exist between children's families and early childhood settings such as the learning center or preschool.

Each family has its own values and ways of doing things. The home atmosphere is the child's first social experience. Coming into a center or preschool—with its different expectations, rules, and styles of adult-child interaction—is a major shift in children's lives at a time when they are learning basic things about how the world works and how to belong.

2. It is most helpful when children experience similar attitudes and expectations of behavior at home and in the early childhood setting. When the expectations in the two places are significantly different, children may have difficulty relating to different sets of values and expectations in the different parts of their lives.

3. Communication between parents and early childhood program staff is very important. It can help to create more understanding and cooperation between a child's home and the early childhood program.

It's important for the well-being of children that we communicate with their parents in ways that are informed, effective, and positive.

It's important for the well-being of children that we communicate with their parents in ways that are informed, effective, and positive.

Teachers and caregivers need to be skilled in communicating with parents as well as children. Sometimes, because of our training, it's easy to approach teacher-parent relationships believing the teacher is the expert who knows best about children, and that it is our job to tell parents how they can become more effective. This attitude will not develop the atmosphere of cooperation necessary for working together.

Attitudes have a big effect on parent-teacher cooperation. For example, some teachers may believe they are in charge of the classroom, and therefore do not want any interference from parents. This belief can take many forms:

• "I am in control. Others should respect that and defer to me."

• "I am in charge and I don't want to be challenged by anyone."

• "The children make so many demands. I can't deal with the demands of the parents as well."

Parents can also have beliefs that cause problems, such as:

• "I'm the parent and you're the teacher. You work for me."

• "I am entitled to tell you directly and exactly how to deal with my child."

Beliefs and attitudes like these can sometimes make it difficult to form a strong parent-teacher partnership. Yet in the interests of children, the relationship between parents and teachers needs to be cooperative and free of attempts from either side to control the other.

> *Four-year-old Stewart's mother believes he needs firm discipline in order to behave. She tells his teacher, "If Stewart misbehaves, I give you permission to slap his hand." Stewart's teacher explains that she never uses physical discipline with the children (and isn't allowed to do so because of licensing regulations). The teacher explains that she tries to prevent most misbehavior by making her expectations clear and requiring children to show respect for each other. Stewart's mother isn't convinced these methods will work, but she thanks the teacher for explaining her discipline policy.*

As teachers, it is an important part of our job to lead the way in initiating teacher-parent understanding and cooperation. A good practice for teachers is to regularly think about and recognize any personal beliefs or feelings on their part which may be acting as blocks in relationships with parents and others. The best way to do this is by being open and sensitive to feedback from other teachers and parents. If you truly listen, people will tell you what you need to know.

Teachers also need to listen closely and understand what parents are communicating about parenting, their child, and how *they* see the teacher-child relationship. Sometimes it is helpful to use reflective listening—to paraphrase back to the parent what it is you are hearing him or her say. That way, the parent knows you have mentally registered the specific nature of their concern. (See Chapter 2 for a detailed explanation of reflective listening.)

Three-year-old Alaina's mom worries about her daughter because she has frequent asthma attacks. She asks the teacher to keep Alaina inside and quiet during gym time.

Alaina's teacher rephrases the mother's concern: "I understand. You're afraid that if Alaina runs around outside she might have an asthma attack." Then the teacher presents her view. She explains that it is important for Alaina's social development for her to be part of the group. She asks Alaina's mother to talk to the child's doctor and bring medical guidelines on the amount of activity Alaina is capable of doing, and what to do in case of an asthma attack at school. She also assures Alaina's mother that she will pay special attention to her daughter to be sure she doesn't overexert herself.

Once Alaina's mother knows that the teacher will be monitoring Alaina, she gradually becomes less protective.

Understanding Parents

It is important to remember that most parents love their children very much and want to be good parents. This is true regardless of how busy, preoccupied, or different in style from you they may be. In this section we are going to discuss some personality dynamics which may result in communication problems between teachers and parents. In "Just for You" in Chapter 2, you examined your own personality priorities. Like teachers, parents too have personality characteristics or *priorities* that influence their behavior and interactions with others.

Understanding Personality Priorities

Many of the beliefs both parents and teachers hold are rooted in their basic personality priorities. Personality priorities are formed by the ways people see the world, and how they believe they must act in order to belong and be accepted by others. These are the same fundamental beliefs we as teachers are helping young children develop in healthy ways. In adults, the beliefs and priorities have already been established.

Understanding personality priorities can help us look at behavior patterns that both parents and teachers use. Once you recognize a personality priority tendency, you will have a better understanding of how the person approaches situations in seeking to belong and work with others.

Personality priorities include tendencies toward:

- Control

- Perfectionism

- Pleasing

- Being a victim

- Being a martyr

While these categories do not tell us everything there is to know about a person, they do provide helpful ways to think about how we and others may approach many aspects of life.

Control. A person with this priority has a strong control need and believes he or she must be in charge and get his or her own way in order to make things work out right. This can be effective when the person is problem oriented and organized. People with a control priority are able to make decisions effectively—making choices and planning things comes naturally to them. But too much control can also turn relationships into power conflicts. When dealing with a teacher or parent who has a control priority, people are likely to feel challenged. This may lead them to resist the person, or to feel resentful. Eventually, the people may seek to avoid these feelings by avoiding the controller. This does not make for productive teacher-parent relationships.

> *The teacher in the toddler room feels it is important for her children to behave differently from the infants. When they graduate to the toddler room, she insists they eat only table foods, with no mashed or strained foods. A few children have trouble with the chunkier table foods, but the teacher refuses to respond to the requests from parents for a more gradual transition. The teacher's response is, "They'll eat when they get hungry. Toddlers are picky eaters anyway."*

The same kind of difficulty could arise at home. If a parent with controlling tendencies was handling food transitions in this way, it might result in a hungry and cranky child at school during the day.

By being aware of the control priority either in themselves or in parents, teachers can build on the positive characteristics of the priority—such as making decisions and organizing well.

Perfectionism. A person with this priority believes the way to control self and others is by being perfect.

169

> Robert, the teacher in the three-year-old room, always has the neatest bulletin boards in the center. Fall leaves give way to pumpkins, which in turn give way to turkeys. All of the children's projects look the same. When the director asks Robert about this, he says, "I help them do projects so they won't look messy. It's important to make a good impression for the parents."

The relationship between parents and teachers needs to be cooperative and free of attempts from either side to control the other.

It is only as Robert learns to accept imperfection and encourage the children's individual efforts that he can become more effective as a teacher.

People with a perfectionism priority feel it's important to be at their best at all times. They are often competent and capable people. They are achievement oriented—holding themselves and others to high standards, paying great attention to detail, and always striving to improve. These can be positive attributes to the degree that the person is doing a good job and working towards achievable goals without demanding perfection.

But parents or teachers with a perfectionism priority may put pressure on children, themselves, and others—wanting each skill and situation to live up to their expectations of perfection. This attitude can keep other people at a distance. A person with the perfectionism priority is often overconcerned about making mistakes, and tends to set impossible goals for self and others. This tends to promote feelings of inadequacy when unable to meet such expectations of perfection. These feelings can be disruptive to relationships, and a source of anxiety for both children and adults.

It may be helpful when talking to perfectionist parents to focus on their children's successes. Teachers and parents with perfectionism priorities need to remember, for the children's sake, that all children develop gradually, make mistakes, and have setbacks in the process.

Pleasing. A person with the priority of pleasing believes the way to work well with others is to please people—at all costs. When other people first encounter the pleaser's attitude of concern and involvement, they usually respond positively. However, people can get tired of the pleaser's constant need for approval. And in the end, a person with this tendency often grows weary of feeling that she or he has to constantly try to please others.

> *Malita tries to be responsive to all parental requests. When four-year-old Felipe's mother asks that he be allowed to rest instead of napping, she moves his cot next to her desk and hands him books during naptime. Gradually, she begins to resent this intrusion on her quiet time, but she doesn't know what to say to Filipe's mother, since she has already agreed to the arrangement.*

Teachers or parents with a priority of pleasing may run themselves ragged—trying to please children, teachers, spouses, and their own inner expectations all the time. Also, pleasers often do not express their own concerns, doubts, or questions in situations, and therefore their needs often go unmet. Parents who want to please may hesitate to share concerns. Teachers working with parents who have the priority of pleasing will want to ask many open-ended questions to draw out the parents' concerns.

Being a victim. People who tend towards this priority believe someone else is responsible for their situation. When things do not go well, the victim always thinks it is someone else's fault. This person seeks to get service and sympathy from others. People often tend to avoid someone with a victim priority because that person usually has low self-esteem and low self-respect.

> *At the beginning of the year, Rachael mentions at a parents' meeting she thinks it would be nice if a group of parents would get together to provide seasonal parties for the children during the year. As December draws near, one of the parents asks Rachael if there are any plans for a holiday party. Rachael replies, "Nobody arranged for one. I told parents last fall they'd have to get together and plan a party. Now it seems they've dropped the ball on me. But I can't handle a party all by myself."*

Teachers need to view each child as part of a unique network of relationships, including the child's family, early childhood staff, and other important people in the child's life.

Adults can display feelings of inadequacy, just as children do. When teachers encounter parents with a tendency towards the victim priority, it is helpful to recognize that the parents have become discouraged. Adults who tend towards the victim priority may use their discouragement and inadequacy to get others to excuse them from functioning—or to put others at their service. In working with such parents, it is important to encourage their self-esteem and contributions in a positive way. Teachers need to guard against giving up on efforts to maintain cooperative relationships with discouraged parents.

Being a martyr. Where the victim blames others, the martyr feels overburdened, and thinks people expect too much. People

171

with this priority are often seen as being very responsible—and they often are. But people tend to grow tired of martyrs' many complaints about how much they do and how much they suffer.

> *Clem's classroom is noisier and messier than the other class-rooms in the center. When parents politely bring up their concerns about the noise level, Clem says, "I'm sorry, but I've got too many children to supervise, and not enough help. I can't be everywhere at once."*

A parent who has a martyr priority may offer complaining excuses when asked to assist with field trips, provide snacks, or other cooperative parent-teacher activities. This parent just can't do whatever it is, because he or she is not well, is over-worked, or has a spouse who doesn't help at home. However, people with tendencies toward the martyr priority are often aware of what needs to be done, and usually do feel a sense of responsi-bility under all the excuses.

In working with parents who appear to have either victim or martyr priorities, keep the focus on the children's needs. Use reflective listening to show you hear parents' difficulties. Then be clear about the issue: "I know it's hard to be so busy. That's why we call on all parents to help, so no one has to do too much."

Whether we consider the behavior of parents or ourselves, seek-ing to understand personality priorities can help us work effec-tively with parents and co-workers toward our common goal—the well-being of children.*

Interacting with Parents

Children come to school with attitudes that are heavily influ-enced by the values and attitudes at home.[2] Teachers need to view each child as part of a unique network of relationships, including the child's family, early childhood staff, and other important people in the child's life.

Initial Contacts with Parents

The first contact we make with parents and children can have a strong influence on later relationships. People form lasting impressions and make decisions about one another within the first few minutes of meeting.

---

*For more information on personality priorities, see: Don Dinkmeyer, *The Basics of Understanding Your Lifestyle* (Coral Springs, FL: CMTI Press, 1991).

Communication with parents helps us understand
more about the children we serve.

In your first contact with parents, it's a good idea to listen and understand their views. Don't attempt to communicate your own point of view right away. At this point, communicate by listening and hearing parents' beliefs, feelings, goals, and values. If parents first establish confidence in you as a listener, they will be better able to hear your communications with them later.

Donna, the toddler teacher, meets with parents of each of the children who will be transferring to her room from the infant room. Donna begins the meeting by saying, "I want to learn as much about your child as I can, so I can ease the transition to the toddler room. You know your child. Would you be willing to answer some questions for me?"

"What are some of his favorite activities?
"What toys does she play with at home?
"Is there anything he's afraid of?
"Is she beginning to learn to dress herself?
"Have you started toilet training yet?
"What do you want me to know about your child?"

Donna encourages the parents to talk about their child. She takes notes and asks follow-up questions. She ends the meeting by thanking the parents for their help and tells them she will give them feedback on how their son or daughter is doing in the toddler room.

Once you have listened carefully to parents, take the opportunity to communicate the rules that exist in your program and in your relationship with parents and children. It's helpful to share a brief list of rules that help parents understand your expectations and how they can most effectively relate to you. Later, follow-up reminders may be necessary when specific situations begin to arise with the children.

Five-year-old Emilio brings a squirt gun to school in his backpack. His teacher explains to him that she doesn't allow children to play with guns in the classroom. The next day, the gun is in the backpack again. When Emilio's dad comes to pick him up, the teacher mentions her rule about no guns in school. Emilio's father says, "I played with toy guns when I was growing up and I turned out fine."

Emilio's teacher smiles and says, "I know. I did too. But we were playing outside with a few children. Here I have to contend with twenty children inside. Gun play gets rowdy and noisy. I'd like Emilio to keep his squirt gun at home. Would you help remind him, please?"

In your first contacts with parents, it's important to communicate that you are empathic—that you understand their feelings, are concerned, and care about their children. It is equally important to communicate your values and limits.

Informal Contacts with Parents

During the year, teachers have many informal contacts with parents. Even though the conversations may be brief (often only a minute or two), it is important to be aware that in these brief contacts, strong and sometimes lasting impressions are created. A teacher's hurried attitude, lack of eye contact, or failure to listen to a parent can convey a lack of caring and understanding to parents. This impression may be generalized by the parent into a judgment about your whole approach to children and to parents.

Your relationship with parents will ideally be open and warm—one that stimulates mutual trust. To develop such a relationship, we suggest that you:

- Know the parents' names and greet them by name.

- Begin conversations by sharing something positive about their child.

- Pay attention to them by maintaining eye contact and listening closely.

- Take a moment to write brief personal comments on any general letters you send home to parents.

- Make calls from time to time to express something positive to parents about their child—especially parents you don't get to talk to often at the center.[3]

In your interaction with parents, it's important to be sensitive to confidentiality. When an issue of concern comes up, avoid discussing it in front of other parents or the child. You can show discretion by suggesting that you'd like to meet the parent at another time for a discussion. Or you can offer to call them, and either discuss the matter on the phone or use the call to set up an individual meeting time.

Start with the positive—on a regular basis. Parents need to feel they are in touch with you frequently about their child. If you are in the habit of sharing typical and positive observations with parents about their children, things will be more comfortable if you need to talk over a problem at some point.

This kind of regular and positive communication can take place in quick conversations or brief notes:

- "Holly and Rebecca played together most of the day today. They really enjoy building things together. They're becoming good friends."

- "Antony climbed to the top of the slide today and said, 'I'm as big as the trees! I can almost touch the clouds!'"

Positive communication like this lays the groundwork for establishing a relationship of parent-teacher cooperation. This can be especially important when there is an issue of concern to discuss.

Parents appreciate when teachers acknowledge
their children's positive traits.

Deal with problems matter-of-factly. Parents have a big emotional investment in their children. It is understandable that they may feel upset if you indicate their child has a problem. In these situations, it's important to focus on the problem without becoming angry at the child or the situation. *"Can we talk now or sometime soon about helping June work on cooperating?"*—sounds very different than—*"I need to talk to you about June's stubbornness. It's really causing a problem."*

When talking with parents about children's problems, communicate clearly that *all* children experience some problems in the process of maturing.[4] Many problems are developmental and can be seen in perspective. When parents ask you in various ways, "Am I a good parent?" you can respond to them first by reassuring them that their love and concern are two important ingredients for their child's well-being. Go on from there to help them explore alternative ways of parenting. You can support and encourage them for recognizing their need for information. If you provide parent education classes, you can encourage them to attend.

It will not be possible for you to answer all the questions you may get at different times from parents. You may often be asked questions that are beyond your current range of information about children. When this happens, don't attempt to answer the question on your own. It may be helpful if you suggest some good references for parents to read. You can refer them to their pediatrician, suggesting that they ask for information or referral to child psychologists, hearing, vision, and speech therapists, and other specialists as needed.

Communicate effectively and respectfully. Parents and teachers need to be responsive to each other. Teachers want parents to understand their assumptions about effective early childhood education, how they function with the child at school—and why. For this reason, teachers send parent-child training information to parents. Parents can be very helpful by reinforcing at home what their child is learning at school.

In the same way, teachers need to be responsive to home-related issues of concern to the parents.

Three-year-old Jimmy and his mother come into the preschool room. Jimmy's teacher has noticed that his mother tends to do things for him and baby him. His teacher wants to encourage Jimmy to be more independent, so she says, "Hi, Jimmy! Why don't you show your mom how you unzip your jacket and hang it on the hook." Jimmy unzips his jacket, takes it off, and hangs it up. He turns to his mother with a smile. His mother says, "Jimmy, I'm proud of you. You're getting to be a big boy."

Ten-month-old Carlotta has a rash on her face. Carlotta's mom mentions the rash to her teacher and says she's not sure what's causing it. Carlotta's teacher says, "Rashes can happen for lots of reasons. It might be due to teething, or Carlotta might be allergic to a particular food, or even the detergent used on the crib sheets. Why don't you have the pediatrician look at it, and then if she wants, we can experiment with eliminating certain foods from Carlotta's diet."

Children develop well if their experiences at home and at the center relate to each other in ways that reinforce growth in both places. We can help children by being aware of their home lives, and by working with parents to develop continuity between the children's experiences at home and at the center. We can use our informal contacts with parents as an opportunity to use and model respect, encouragement, clear communication, and problem-solving skills.

Writing Encouraging Notes to Parents

We know encouragement is one of the most effective methods a teacher or parent can use in working with a child.[5] Encouragement also helps increase parents' confidence and active involvement in helping their children grow.

As a teacher, you can be most encouraging when you are familiar with the things a child believes and thinks, and when you understand the viewpoint of his parents. Two-way communication with parents can help you gain insight into the family world that influences the child's beliefs about what will make him important and accepted. Communication with parents and caregivers also helps you recognize the relationship patterns between adults and the children at home. And it can shed light on the characteristic behavior patterns of the child.

When talking with parents about children's problems, communicate clearly that all children experience some problems in the process of maturing.

In everything they do, teachers need to look for any strength, asset, or opportunity for giving recognition to the behavior of the child.[6] Recognition of the child's progress and efforts reaps a double reward when both the parent and the child are encouraged by it.

As part of building a good basis for teacher-parent communication, you may want to send home regular Happy Grams—brief, encouraging notes about a child's progress and cooperation. Parents will begin to anticipate that you know positive things about their child, as well as things that need improvement. They will begin to see you as a significant person in the life of their child, and your ideas will become respected input.

Happy Grams

When recognized and noted by teachers, these are all welcome news to parents.

- An increase in motor skills

- A move towards independence by the child in feeding or other self-care

- Growing verbal abilities

- Learning to relate effectively with others

It's important to write encouraging notes in your own words, reflecting your way of looking at the child, yourself, and the parents. Encouraging words help to stimulate cooperation and parental feedback. Examples are: "improving," "more cooperative," "making an effort," "willing to try," "I'm glad," and "thank you."

When you write encouraging notes to parents, identify specific areas where the child is making progress, and deal with these instances in a very concrete way, avoiding exaggerated praise. Instead, encourage movement and effort. Here are some examples:

Dear Mr. Smith,

Loretta has been doing a good job of remembering to use her words instead of fists when she is angry. I commented on her self-control today. When another child grabbed Loretta's doll, she said, "That's mine," instead of hitting. I'm pleased to see her starting to solve problems with words.

———

Dear Ms. Brady,

Cassandra is practicing counting from 1 to 10 at school. Would you be willing to help her practice counting objects at home? Perhaps she could count the doors and windows in your apartment, or the plates and glasses on the table at dinner time. Thanks for your help.

A Happy Gram can brighten a parent's day.

How to Communicate With Parents About Problems

Communicating about problems is unavoidable. By following some simple guidelines, you'll learn to make the process easier and more effective.

Model effective relationship skills. Modeling is a powerful form of communication. As an early childhood teacher, you have special training in understanding children and methods of relating with them effectively. When parents communicate well with you, and watch you model effective ways of relating to children, they can develop a better understanding of their children and how the school program works.

Be clear and positive. When you talk to parents, communicate with them in clear, straightforward language. It's more important to tell them why specific playground activities are valuable, for example, than to talk in general or abstract terms about "opportunities that contribute to the child's well-being."

When you are going to talk with parents about problems:

1. Begin by talking about something that has been going well with the child, or any positive behavior you have observed.

2. Talk about the problem that is of concern to you.

3. Describe the problem in a way that helps the parents understand *specifically* what is happening, and share some hunches or guesses about why it's happening.

4. Describe some solutions you have tried, and ask for any ideas they may have.

Madeline's mother often dresses three-and-a-half-year-old Madeline in frilly dresses for school. Madeline feels anxious about getting her dresses dirty doing art projects or out on the playground. Madeline's teacher writes her mother a note: "Madeline loves to draw with crayons. I have noticed she is sometimes reluctant to try other art projects that are messier because she worries about getting her dresses dirty. I've offered her a big smock, and that seems to help. Can we talk about this one day soon?"

The next day, Madeline's mother talks to the teacher at the school and says, "I didn't know she was worried about getting dirty. Do you think I should dress her in pants?" The teacher replies, "Most of the girls wear pants or casual jumpers. Why don't you try it, and we'll see if she feels freer to experiment."

In working with parents, be sensitive to the most effective way of making suggestions. If you come across to parents as an authority who knows more than the parent does, you will most probably encounter resistance. When you have a suggestion to make regarding something the child is doing, or something you have observed in the parent-child relationship, you can begin by finding out whether the parents are interested in hearing from you on this topic.

Communicate any ideas you have to share in a tentative manner. You might say, "I have an idea about what's happening with regard to _____. Would you like to talk about it?" That gives them a chance to respond or to withdraw. If they want to talk about it, you might take the next step by saying, "I have some ideas. . . . Would you like to hear them?" or, "I have the impression that . . ." Develop an atmosphere of mutual respect in which you and the parents explore ideas together. Once you establish this expectation, you can discuss the purpose of some of the interactions you have noticed and talk about some other ways the parent might be successful with the child.

Four-year-old Jeanna's teacher has noticed she spends a lot of time lately undressing the baby dolls and giggling about them being naked. Jeanna also tries to spy on the boys when they use the bathroom.

The teacher calls Jeanna's mother and asks her when would be a convenient time for them to talk. Jeanna's mother asks the teacher to call back after 8:30, when the children are in bed. The teacher does so and begins the phone conversation by saying, "Thank you for setting aside time to talk with me. Jeanna is so friendly and lively—she is a lot of fun to have in our group." "That's nice to hear," replies Jeanna's mother. Jeanna's teacher then says, "Lately, Jeanna seems very curious about the difference between boys and girls."

"What makes you say that?" Jeanna's mother asks. Jeanna's teacher describes what she has observed and says, "I think she's looking for some answers and she's not sure where to find them. I have a good children's book on human bodies. Would you like me to loan it to you to read with Jeanna?"

Jeanna's mother says, "I'm really glad you called like this. I've noticed she's curious, but I haven't known what to say. I'd like to borrow the book. Thank you."

Communicate any ideas you have to share in a tentative manner. Develop an atmosphere of mutual respect in which you and the parent are exploring ideas together.

If a child's parent is not ready to hear about a problem or concern, it may be better to wait until a time when the parent is more ready. Effective discussions are based on the understanding that both parents and teachers want to solve a problem, without placing blame.

Parent-Teacher Conferences

It is helpful to set up a regular schedule of conferences with parents several times a year. Conferences allow you to meet and talk about the needs and development of each child. They create

You and Your Relationships

It may be a little unsettling to think about yourself in terms of the personality priorities we have discussed in this chapter. At first glance, none of them may seem to apply to you. But it can be valuable to think about them as tendencies. Look for places in your relationships where the priorities do reflect feelings you experience, or ways you are likely to handle situations.

Remember, no priority can define a person entirely—but getting an understanding of your personality priority tendencies can be most valuable in assessing your attitudes, relationships, and experiences with others.

good home-school communication and provide opportunities for small concerns to be aired before they can grow into big ones.

When possible, have both parents—or other concerned adults—attend the conferences. As many parents work during the day, it may be necessary to hold conferences in the evening. If parents are divorced, ask them whether it is agreeable to attend together. If not, you may need to consider separate conferences.

When dealing with parents of a child who is cooperative and doing well in your group, conferences are usually not a problem. However, meetings with parents of children with problem behavior are often approached with great concern by both teachers and parents. It's important to make all conferences, and especially this kind, part of an intentional, positive parent involvement program.

Preparing for the Conference

There are a number of ways to create a good atmosphere for parent-teacher conferences. One is to lay groundwork ahead of time, through the kind of informal notes and parent contacts we have been discussing.

Keeping track of observations. Many teachers find it is helpful to track children's growth and changes by keeping a file for each child. You may want to spend some time on a regular basis observing and making brief notes on each child's interests, responses, participation in activities, social skills, and changes. Date each observation and drop it into the file so you'll have written information to depend on when you prepare a written report for parents at conference time.

Your program may also require you to complete formal observations or assessments of each child's interests and skills. Making observations and taking notes over a period of time can help you interpret what a more formal evaluation might indicate. You may also be able to notice certain patterns in a child's behavior by tracking your observations in this way.

Setting the agenda. When you ask a parent to meet with you for a conference, it is important to be thoroughly prepared. Have a clear plan about what you are going to accomplish in the meeting. Certainly you will be interested in winning the parent's cooperation, but what specific points do you want to make? Are you interested in creating a more relaxed atmosphere at home? Do you want the parent to ease the pressure on the child? What is it you have in mind?

The progress report. At all conferences, parents should be given some information about children's positive and encouraging behaviors, as well as other issues. Prepare a written progress report for the parents to read at the beginning of the conference. This can be a very simple, half-page or one page evaluation that includes:

- A summary of the child's progress

- The strengths of the child

- Any concerns about the child's progress or behaviors

- Solutions and ways you have been effective up to this point

- Your request for additional ideas, suggestions and cooperation

When you are setting up the conference schedule, be sure to allow enough time for the parent to read and digest this short report.

If you make a phone call to set up a special conference with a parent, be sure to mention the child's strengths and things that are going well at the present time. With this groundwork, the conference will feel less like a "report card session" and more like a joint meeting for positive, shared exploration about the development and well-being of the child.

The Conference

After getting comfortable, ask the parent to read your progress report on the child. Ask for the parent's reactions. Is there anything in these comments she would like to discuss? If the parent appears upset, use reflective listening, indicating the feelings and beliefs you are hearing. Explain anything that is not understood. Clarify how you see the child's performance and what positive outcomes you think might come out of this meeting.

Conferences foster good home-school communication and provide opportunities for small concerns to be aired before they can grow into big ones.

> *Michiko is an active, busy four-year-old who will turn five in August. His parents plan to send him to kindergarten in the fall, but his teacher has noticed that his fine motor skills are not very well developed. Michiko's teacher decides to collect some samples of his work to share with his parents. Over a two-week period she asks Michiko to draw a person, write his name, cut on a straight and curvy line, and glue some paper strips into rings. She saves these projects and arranges a conference time with Michiko's parents.*
>
> *The teacher begins the conference by pointing out some of Michiko's strengths. He's enthusiastic about block building, he loves to sing, and he likes to climb and run outdoors. The teacher then mentions that Michiko usually avoids art projects and table toys unless he's encouraged to try them. She mentions he gets frustrated easily when he's using scissors or doing a puzzle, and he often gives up. She shows the parents samples of Michiko's work and talks about how it compares to that of other children who are about the same age.*
>
> *Michiko's parents ask what they should do. His teacher explains they have several options. They might choose to work at home with Michiko on his cutting and drawing skills. If so, she'd be glad to suggest ideas for activities. She also points out Michiko is one of the youngest children in the class, and he might need a little more time to mature. She suggests they consider the possibility of delaying Michiko's entrance to kindergarten or placing him in a small class where he can get extra attention.*

In some instances, a parent may ask to have a conference. In these conferences, follow the parent's lead and discuss the issues that concern him. Hear the feelings and beliefs and use reflective listening, especially if the parent is angry or upset.

In all conferences, summarize and state your positions with clear I-messages. If there is some confusion, brainstorm with the parent.

Three-and-a-half-year-old Denzel's speech is hard to understand. His teacher frequently needs to ask him to repeat what he's said, and this seems to frustrate Denzel. When his speech doesn't appear to be improving after two months at the center, the teacher calls Denzel's father and asks him to come in for a conference.

Denzel's father looks worried when the teacher tells him that Denzel's speech is hard to understand. He confronts the teacher by saying, "Are you trying to tell me Denzel is slow or dumb?"

The teacher replies, "Not at all. I'm just saying that Denzel has difficulty pronouncing some sounds. Would you be willing to consult a speech therapist for an evaluation? A number of other children I've worked with have been to speech therapists, and it's remarkable how quickly their speech can improve when they get practice and help in making certain sounds. If you'd like, we could arrange for the therapist to observe Denzel when he's in school talking to his classmates."

Denzel's father relaxes a little and confides, "I used to get teased about my speech when I was younger. The other kids called me stupid. I don't want that happening to Denzel. Could you recommend a speech therapist?"

In some conferences you may clearly identify that you and the parents have conflicting objectives. For example, you may know the child is engaging in a power contest at school and at home. You may want the parents to withdraw from power contests as you do at your center. Instead, they may want to force the child to do things their way. In a short period of time, you may find yourself in another power contest—with the parents. You need to clarify why you want the child to learn from the consequences of behavior. Parents will not always understand children the same way you do. They might believe the child should not become more independent, but instead should continue to remain dependent upon them. They may resent your methods or your assessment of the child.

You cannot expect that parents will always come around to share your point of view in a conference. But when you present your concerns respectfully and in the spirit of helping the child, parents are likely to think about what you say. You may see results later, despite initial resistance.

When there has been some misbehavior on the part of a child, always:

1. Present a brief description of the situation that occurred.

2. State your perceptions of the child's goal of misbehavior.

3. Inform the parents of your response to the misbehavior and your attempts to focus on the child's strengths.

4. Find out about the child's relationship with the parents.

5. Find out about birth order. Knowing whether a child is the oldest, middle, youngest, or only child will provide clues in understanding behavior.[7]

6. Explore alternatives that may help the child get along better at school (and at home, if appropriate).

7. Get a commitment to a solution parents and teachers can cooperate on, and set a time for evaluation.

A strong parent education program is an essential part of an early childhood program. Early childhood teachers can be effective leaders in setting up educational programs for parents.

Three-year-old Luke is physically aggressive. He angers easily and strikes back quickly. The teacher's attempts to stop Luke's aggressive behavior with time-outs and withdrawal of privileges have met with limited success. Luke's teacher asks his mother to come in for a conference. After visiting with her about the areas Luke has made progress in, the teacher brings up the physical aggression. She tells Luke's mother what methods she has tried, and asks her for ideas and suggestions.

Luke's mother says he is a rough and tumble child. He wrestles and fights a lot with his older brothers. She also says that she sometimes spanks Luke because she gets so frustrated with his misbehavior. Luke's teacher talks with his mother about why it's important for Luke to see other people solving problems by negotiating instead of fighting. She suggests enlisting Luke's older brothers as helpers who can give Luke positive recognition when he uses words instead of fists.

At the end of the conference, the teacher promises to call Luke's mother in two weeks to discuss how the plan is working and to make any necessary adjustments. Luke's mother thanks the teacher for her suggestions.

Parent Education Groups

The early childhood years are crucial in developing a child's self-worth, confidence, skills, and feelings of responsibility. A strong parent education program is an essential part of an early childhood program. Early childhood teachers can be effective leaders in setting up educational programs for parents. Ideally, parent education and involvement would be a required part of the total early childhood education experience.

Recognize that very few parents have had special education or training for the job of being a parent. Many people assume effective parenting is something that is acquired incidentally and naturally. In fact, parents benefit greatly from being participants in parent education groups. Such groups give them an opportunity to learn about and discuss parenting challenges—and to give and get support in their parenting.

There are a number of different approaches to parent education. There are also many ways of getting parents involved in parent education experiences. Early childhood staff members need to recognize the importance of this part of their work and make it a regular and consistent part of the education they offer to families. In many instances, the educator for parents will be a director, teacher, or a specialist who is not on the staff. It is desirable for the parent educator to have a thorough understanding of the theory and process of the parent education program being taught. Parent educators also need group leadership skills.

There are a variety of structured programs and books available for parent study. We recommend *Early Childhood STEP* [8] because the program's theory and process parallel information presented in *Teaching and Leading Children*. The course focuses on the following topics:

- Understanding young children and their behavior

- Building self-esteem

- Communication with children

- Helping young children learn cooperation

- Effective discipline

- Nurturing emotional and social development

The Importance of Teaching

As early childhood teachers, we are privileged to share with parents the responsibility of helping children develop at a crucial period of their lives. Parents bring their children to us looking for the best we have to offer. By maintaining strong home-school relationships, good communication, effective parent-teacher conferences, and parent education opportunities, we share our professional commitment with parents and provide children with the best early childhood experience possible.

Teachers and parents share a common goal: to raise children who are honest, responsible, cooperative, respectful of others, and courageous. By encouraging children to develop these skills, teachers provide them with the tools they need to be happy, successful, and capable of enjoying life.

Notes

1. Douglas Powell, *Families and Early Childhood Programs* (Washington D.C.: NAEYC, Research Monographs of the National Association for the Education of Young Children Vol. 3, 1989), pp. 23-51.

2. Stephanie Feeney, Doris Christensen, and Eva Moravcik, *Who Am I In The Lives of Children? (4th ed.)* (New York: Merrill/Macmillan, 1991).

3. Elizabeth Morgan, "Talking with Parents When Concerns Come Up," *Young Children*, January, 1989.

4. Morgan, "Talking with Parents When Concerns Come Up."

5. There is an entire work devoted to encouragement: Don Dinkmeyer and Lewis Losoncy, *The Encouragement Book: Becoming a Positive Person* (Englewood Cliffs, NJ: Prentice Hall, 1980).

6. See Dinkmeyer and Losoncy: *The Encouragement Book.*

7. For more information about the effects of birth order in children's lives, see Don Dinkmeyer, Gary D. McKay, and James S. Dinkmeyer, *Parenting Young Children* (Circle Pines, MN: American Guidance Service, 1989), pp. 25-26.

8. For more information about *Early Childhood STEP*, contact American Guidance Service, 4201 Woodland Road, Circle Pines, MN 55014-1796. Phone: (612) 786-4343.

Problem Situations

Infant. David is an active child, big for his age, who has been in Marcia's infant room since he was ten months old. He was a beginning crawler at that time, and now, at fifteen months, is showing no interest in walking. If Marcia pulls David up and holds his hands, he is able to stand, but Marcia hasn't seen him pull himself up on his own. The other children Marcia has cared for have all begun to attempt to walk before fifteen months. Marcia knows that some children develop these large muscle skills later than others. Marcia decides to talk to David's father to learn a little more about David's history and hear if he has any concerns.

1. How might Marcia approach this subject with David's father?

2. If David's father seems concerned, what might Marcia do?

3. If David's father does not seem concerned, what might Marcia do?

4. What should Marcia do if David does not begin to walk within the next three months?

Toddler. Two-and-a-half-year-old Sasha is an only child. Her mother and stepfather have recently placed her in Mrs. Letrec's Montessori school. While Mrs. Letrec wants to stimulate children's creativity and curiosity, she does not want to push them or force them into unnatural learning situations. Sasha's parents are proud of their daughter's talents and intelligence. Mrs. Letrec has noticed that they usually want Sasha to "perform" after school, often asking Sasha to "read" them a story the children heard during the day, sing, dance, or recite something for them. Sasha's parents are very loving, but their demands on their daughter seem excessive. Mrs. Letrec has observed that most days when she is picked up, Sasha begins to behave wild and contrary as soon as her parents begin to pressure her.

1. How might Mrs. Letrec approach this subject with Sasha's parents?

2. If Sasha's parents do not agree with Mrs. Letrec's concerns, what else can Mrs. Letrec do?

Preschooler. Four-year-old Jeremiah has been a consistently lively and energetic child for the entire year his teacher, Miss Jessie, has known him. During the past two or three weeks, Miss Jessie has noticed an abrupt change in Jeremiah's general mood. He has taken to crying and clinging to his mother when she drops him off and to his teacher after his mother leaves. Jeremiah also seems unusually aggressive with other children; this week Miss Jessie has had to remove him from conflicts with other children several times.

1. Why might it be useful for Miss Jessie to talk with Jeremiah's mother about her son's behavior change?

2. How might Miss Jessie approach this situation?

Chart 6

Communication with Parents

Effective	Ineffective
1. Listen to the parents' beliefs and feelings in order to understand their beliefs about their child.	1. Tell the parents your beliefs about children, but do not take their ideas seriously.
2. In your early contacts with parents, share with them a brief list of your rules and expectations.	2. Do not share your classroom rules with parents.
3. In talking with parents about a problem with a child, begin by talking about any positive behavior you have noted.	3. In talking with parents regarding a problem with a child, begin immediately focusing on the problem and your solution.
4. Send encouraging notes that recognize any change or progress.	4. Encourage only by praising outstanding work.
5. Send Happy Grams to parents.	5. Emphasize the child's mistakes in reporting to parents.
6. Communicate your feelings clearly through I-messages.	6. Let parents know your anger about the child's behavior even though you seem to be attacking them.
7. Develop plans with parents and seek agreement for a plan of action.	7. Make your plans without any discussion with parents.
8. When parents are upset, listen to their feelings.	8. Make quick judgments and develop solutions quickly.
9. Develop a cooperative relationship with parents.	9. Be sure parents know you are in charge.

Applying Your Skills

Set up an individual file folder for each of your children. Spend ten to fifteen minutes a day making observations about the behavior, achievements, and problems of two or three specific children. Jot the observations down and put them in the folders. Using these observations, practice communicating with parents at the beginning and end of the day. Remember to make your comments positive and encouraging. If you observe problems that you would like to talk to parents about at another time, make plans for how and when to open such a discussion.

Things to Consider

While the skills we present have been found to be effective in most cases, you will want to determine a skill's effectiveness in your situation. As you think about this assignment:

• Examine the environment in which you meet with parents. Think about any activities or scheduling factors which may interfere with communication.

• Examine any personal liabilities on your part, such as being easy to anger, talking too much, being demanding, having to be in control, trying to be perfect, or wanting to please.

• Assess your personal resources for communicating effectively. These are qualities or strengths such as a sense of humor, being a good listener, problem solving, tactfulness, or being perceptive about unspoken feelings.

Follow-Up

If your group does not meet again, plan a time to evaluate your efforts with others in your center who have taken the *TLC* class. If the results of the assignment are unsatisfactory, decide how you can modify your approach in the future.

Record Keeping (Optional)

You may find it helpful to log your observations and actions. The following format can be used for your log.

Daily Log   Child's Name:_____

	Parents Contacted	My Comments	Response
Monday			
Tuesday			
Wednesday			
Thursday			
Friday			

1. Teacher-parent relationships are most effective when the attitude fostered by the teacher is one of equality and working together.

2. Listen closely to what parents communicate about parenting and about their children in order to identify the parents' beliefs. Also, be aware of your own beliefs or attitudes which may throw up blocks to effective relationships.

3. Personality priorities are important in understanding both yourself and the parents you work with.

4. Strong tendencies toward priorities of control, perfectionism, pleasing, being a victim, or being a martyr can cause stress and tension when they determine your methods of relating with children and parents.

5. In your first contact with parents, focus on listening and understanding rather than in telling and directing.

6. Once you have carefully listened to parents, share a brief list of your operating rules and expectations with them.

7. It is important to develop common goals and expectations among teachers and parents.

8. Encouragement that focuses on strengths and positive observations is one of the most effective procedures in working with young children and their parents.

9. Encouraging notes to parents can recognize any progress or positive movement. This communicates to the child that he does not have to be perfect—any effort is noteworthy.

10. In talking with parents, do it in an encouraging way. This can be assisted by making inquiries in a tentative manner,("Could it be . . . ?" "Is it possible . . . ?"), focusing on the purpose of the child's behavior and ways to help modify the behavior.

11. By sending home regular Happy Grams which report on the child's progress and cooperation, you help parents to know you recognize positive things about the child.

12. When you are going to talk with a parent about a problem with a child, begin by talking about some things that have been going well. Work to create an atmosphere of cooperation and understanding. Explain clearly how you are handling problem behavior—and why. Maintain an attitude of mutual respect and joint concern for the well-being of the child.

13. By using I-messages, you communicate your feelings clearly and model the process for the parents.

14. Early childhood educators need to provide parent education to support the parents of the children they teach.

Just For You

As you take charge of your beliefs, feelings, and self-worth or self-esteem, you will become more satisfied, enthusiastic, and energized. You will experience states of creative energy and joy more often.

You will become "a courageous person who looks at any situation in terms of possible solutions or actions rather than dangers or threats."* In order to change your perspective on your personal and professional relationships, you need to build your capacities to function more positively and more effectively.

Set aside some daily time for self-affirmation.

Examples of self-affirming statements are:

- "I decide for myself."
- "I am responsible."
- "I can see the positive in any situation."
- "I am capable."
- "I make decisions."
- "I like myself."
- "I have a sense of humor."
- "I am an effective teacher."**

Practice self affirmation by becoming relaxed: Sit with both feet on the floor, hands limp in lap, palms up.

- Close your eyes.
- Take a deep breath through your nose and exhale.
- Continue to relax.
- Take several breaths.

Once you are relaxed, you are ready to say positive affirmations.

- Say to yourself, "I . . . (finish the sentence with your affirmation.)"
- See yourself that way. Believe it.
- Now say a second affirmation: "I . . ." Believe it.
- Say a third affirmation. "I . . ." Believe it.

Go through the sequence of affirmations three times. Believe what you are saying.

---

* Don Dinkmeyer and Lewis Losoncy, *The Encouragement Book: Becoming a Positive Person* (Englewood Cliffs, NJ: Prentice Hall, 1980).
** Don Dinkmeyer, *The Basics of Understanding Your Lifestyle* (Coral Springs, FL: CMTI Press, 1991), p.12.

Appendix A

Child Abuse

Child abuse is a widespread problem that is of concern to all parents and teachers of children. The National Committee for Prevention of Child Abuse (NCPCA) reports that in 1990, there were more than 2.5 million reports of child abuse and neglect in the United States. Children who suffer abuse and neglect often have difficulty learning in school, maintaining friendships, and becoming happy and healthy adults. Because most children spend more time with their teachers than with any other adults outside of their family, it is vital for educators of young children to have an understanding of what child abuse is and their role in identifying and reporting it.

What Is Child Abuse?

The NCPCA identifies and defines four forms of child abuse:[*]

- **Physical abuse**—nonaccidental injury, which may include beatings, violent shaking, human bites, strangulation, suffocation, poisoning, or burns.

- **Neglect**—the failure to provide a child with basic needs, including food, clothing, education, shelter, and medical care; also abandonment and inadequate supervision.

- **Sexual abuse**—the sexual exploitation of a child by an older person, as in rape, incest, fondling of the genitals, exhibitionism, or pornography. It may be done for the sexual gratification of the older person, out of a need for power, or for economic reasons.

- **Emotional maltreatment**—a pattern of behavior that attacks a child's emotional development and sense of self-

---

[*] Taken from Paula Jaudes and Leslie Mitchel, *Physical Child Abuse* (Chicago: National Committee for Prevention of Child Abuse, 1992).

worth, such as constant criticizing, belittling, insulting, manipulation; also, providing no love, support or guidance.

Warning Signs

Educators of young children have an extra challenge in identifying children who are suffering abuse or neglect. Infants and preverbal toddlers lack the language skills necessary to report abuse to their teachers. Even after gaining these skills, children under the age of five are much less likely to directly report abuse to a teacher than are older children. This places even greater importance on the ability of teachers to identify the tacit signs of abuse and neglect in young children.

The NCPCA lists these signs as indicators of possible neglect or abuse.** No one of these signs proves a child has been abused, but when signs appear often and in combination with each other, it should alert the teacher to examine the situation more carefully and to consider the possibility of child abuse.

Signs of physical abuse. Consider the possibility of physical abuse when the child:

* has unexplained burns, bites, bruises, broken bones, or black eyes;
* has fading bruises or other marks noticeable after an absence from the child care center;
* seems frightened of the parents and protests or cries when it is time to go home; or
* shrinks at the approach of adults.

Signs of neglect. Consider the possibility of neglect when the child:

* is frequently absent from the child care center;
* begs or steals food from other children;
* lacks needed medical or dental care, immunizations, or glasses;
* is consistently dirty and has severe body odor; or
* lacks sufficient clothing for the weather.

Signs of sexual abuse. Consider the possibility of sexual abuse when the child:

* has difficulty walking or sitting;
* suddenly refuses to participate in physical activities; or
* demonstrates bizarre, sophisticated, or unusual sexual knowledge or behavior.

** Taken from Diane D. Broadhurst, *Educators, Schools, and Child Abuse* (Chicago: National Committee for Prevention of Child Abuse, 1986).

Signs of emotional maltreatment. Consider the possibility of emotional maltreatment when the child:

- shows extremes in behavior, such as overly compliant or demanding behavior, extreme passivity or aggression;

- is either inappropriately adult (parenting other children, for example) or inappropriately infantile (frequently rocking or head-banging, for example); or

- is delayed in physical or emotional development.

How to Handle Disclosure of Abuse

Many educators fear that children will disclose to them that they have been victimized. Their fear stems from a concern that they may not be able to help the child sufficiently by seeing that the abuse is stopped and the child is safe from further abuse.

In *Educators, Schools, and Child Abuse*, Diane D. Broadhurst presents the following information:

In every state in the United States, in its territories, and in the District of Columbia, educators are required by law to report suspected child abuse. The range of educators mandated to report is broad. It includes principals, teachers, counselors, school nurses, and staff of residential institutions, day care centers and summer camps.

By law a suspicion of child abuse generally means that the reporter has "reasonable cause to believe" or "reasonable cause to know or suspect" that the child has been maltreated. Reporters do *not* have to know that abuse actually took place in order to report. In fact, many laws require that reports be made of circumstances or conditions that could reasonably result in future child abuse—if, for example, one were to learn that a child would be unattended while parents were vacationing.

In most states, reports can be made orally to the mandated agency (usually called the Department of Social Services). Many communities have hot lines to receive telephone reports. In many jurisdictions the law permits teachers and other school personnel to report to the principal or to the principal's designated agent. This person, in turn, is responsible for notifying the appropriate authorities.

Sometimes, educators are reluctant to report suspected child abuse because they do not want to get involved, or they believe that reporting will jeopardize the teacher-pupil relationship, or they fear personal liability. Some educators believe that if a report they make proves erroneous, the child's parents will sue them for libel, slander, defamation of character, or invasion of privacy. Reporting laws provide immunity, however, from civil and criminal liability if the report was made in *good faith*. Good faith simply means an honest belief by the reporter that the child was abused or that the substance of the report, which may be only a suspicion, is valid. The reporter need only have a *reasonable* suspicion that the abuse has occurred. The law does not require proof; it specifically does require reporting of *suspected* child abuse. Proving the case is the responsibility of trained investigators, not the one who reports.

There is little chance that an educator will be successfully sued by a parent for reporting suspected child abuse, unless the report was made maliciously—for example, as part of a personal vendetta by a teacher against a pupil's parent.

The law does impose liability on mandated reporters who *fail* to report suspected child abuse. In an effort to encourage reporting, the laws provide that failure to report is a crime, usually a misdemeanor. Penalties vary by state: some penalties may be as low as a few days in jail, a $10 fine, or both; or penalties may be as high as a year in jail, a $1,000 fine, or both. In most states criminal liability will arise only if the reporter knowingly or willfully failed to report. Educators who fail to report suspected child abuse may be deemed civilly liable for negligent performance of their duties, however, and may be subject to both legal and administrative penalties.

If a child begins to tell you about an incident of abuse during class time, respond by saying, "(Heather), I really want to hear what you have to say. It sounds important, but we can't talk about it right now. You and I can talk about it together when the class is done with this activity." At the time indicated, ask the child to tell you about what happened; don't wait for the child to come to you. If the child doesn't want to repeat the story, don't pressure him or her; tell the child to come and talk with you about it at another time if he or she would like.

Letting the child know all of the following is important:

- The child did the right thing in telling you.
- You believe the child.
- The child is not to blame.
- You are sorry about what happened.
- You will do your best to protect the child and see that the abuse doesn't happen again.
- The child can come again and talk with you about any problem.

Teachers report more cases of abuse than any other mandated reporters. Most schools and child-care institutions have a specific reporting procedure that must be followed when child abuse is suspected. Take the time to familiarize yourself with the reporting policies and procedures of your school or organization.

Appendix B

Resources for Early Childhood Teachers

Development and Guidance

Allen, K. E., and Marotz, L. *Developmental Profiles: Birth to Six.* Albany, NY: Delmar Publishers, Inc., 1989.

Brazelton, T. Berry. *To Listen to a Child: Understanding the Normal Problems of Growing Up.* Reading, MA: Addison-Wesley, 1984.

————. *Toddlers and Parents: A Declaration of Independence.* New York: A Delta Book, 1974.

————. *What Every Baby Knows.* New York: Ballantine Books, 1987.

————. *Working and Caring.* Reading, MA: Addison-Wesley, 1985.

Bredekamp, Sue, ed. *Developmentally Appropriate Practice in Early Childhood Programs Serving Children from Birth Through Age Eight.* Expanded ed. Washington, DC: National Association for the Education of Young Children, 1987.

Cherry, Clare. *Please Don't Sit on the Kids: Alternatives to Punitive Discipline.* Belmont, CA: David S. Lake, 1983.

Chess, Stella, and Thomas, Alexander. *Know Your Child: An Authoritative Guide for Today's Parents.* New York: Basic Books, 1987.

Elkind, David. Miseducation: *Preschoolers at Risk.* New York: Knopf, 1987.

Galinsky, Ellen, and David, Judy. *The Preschool Years: Family Strategies That Work—From Experts and Parents.* New York: Ballantine Books, 1988.

Gartrell, Dan, and Johnson, Nancy, eds. *Developmentally Appropriate Guidance of Young Children.* St. Paul, MN: Minnesota Association for the Education of Young Children, 1991.

Greenberg, P. *Character Development: Encouraging Self-Esteem and Self-Discipline in Infants, Toddlers, and Two-Year-Olds.* Washington, DC: National Association for the Education of Young Children, 1991.

Greenspan, Stanley. *Floor Time.* New York: Scholastic, 1990.

Greenspan, Stanley, and Greenspan, Nancy Thorndike. *First Feelings.* New York: Viking Penguin, 1985.

Hildebrand, Verna. *Guiding Young Children.* 4th ed. New York: Macmillan, 1990.

Mitchell, Grace. *A Very Practical Guide to Discipline with Young Children.* Marshfield, MA: Telshare, 1982.

Nelson, Jan, and Glenn, H. Stephen. *Time Out: Abuses and Effective Uses.* Provo, UT: Sunrise Press, 1991.

Reynolds, Eleanor. *Guiding Young Children: A Child Centered Approach.* Mountain View, CA: Mayfield, 1990.

Surbeck, Elaine, and Kelley, Michael, eds. *Personalizing Care with Infants, Toddlers, and Families.* Wheaton, MD: Association for Childhood Education International, 1990.

White, Burton L. *The First Three Years of Life.* Rev. ed. New York: Prentice Hall, 1985.

Curriculum Resources

Baird, Kristin, and Kile, Marilyn J. *BodyRights: A DUSO Approach to Preventing Sexual Abuse of Children.* Circle Pines, MN: American Guidance Service, 1986.

Breighner, Kathryn, and Rohe, Deborah. *I Am Amazing: A Program Promoting Health, Safety, and Self-Esteem.* Circle Pines, MN: American Guidance Service, 1990.

Davis, Duane E. *My Friends & Me.* Circle Pines, MN: American Guidance Service, 1988.

Dinkmeyer, Don, and Dinkmeyer, Don, Jr. *Developing Understanding of Self and Others* (DUSO-R). Rev. ed. Circle Pines, MN: American Guidance Service, 1982.

Dreyer, Sharon Spredemann. *The Bookfinder.* Vol. 4. Circle Pines, MN: American Guidance Service, 1989.

————. *The Best of Bookfinder.* Circle Pines, MN: American Guidance Service, 1992.

Dunn, Lloyd M., et al. *Peabody Early Experiences Kit (PEEK).* Circle Pines, MN: American Guidance Service, 1976.

Karnes, Merle B. *Fit For Me: Activities for Building Motor Skills in Young Children.* Circle Pines, MN: American Guidance Service, 1992.

————. *Small Wonder!* Levels 1 and 2. Circle Pines, MN: American Guidance Service, 1979, 1981.

Working with Parents

Curran, Dolores. *Working With Parents: Dolores Curran's Guide to Successful Parent Groups.* Circle Pines, MN: American Guidance Service, 1989.

Dinkmeyer, Don; McKay, Gary D.; and Dinkmeyer, James S. *Early Childhood STEP.* Circle Pines, MN: American Guidance Service, 1989. A Spanish-language edition is also available.

Dinkmeyer, Don; McKay, Gary D.; and McKay, Joyce L. *New Beginnings: Skills for Single Parents and Stepfamily Parents—Parent's Manual.* Champaign, IL: Research Press, 1987.

Einstein, Elizabeth, and Albert, Linda. *Strengthening Stepfamilies.* Circle Pines, MN: American Guidance Service, 1986.

Karnes, Merle B. *You and Your Small Wonder.* Vols. 1 and 2. Circle Pines, MN: American Guidance Service, 1982.

Lerman, Saf. *Responsive Parenting.* Circle Pines, MN: American Guidance Service, 1984.

Washburn Child Guidance Center. *EveryDay Matters.* Circle Pines, MN: American Guidance Service, 1991.

Professional Organizations

Association for Childhood Education International (ACEI)
11501 Georgia Avenue, Suite 312
Wheaton, MD 20902-4110
301-942-2443

Child Development Associate (CDA) National
Credentialing Program
Council for Early Childhood Professional Recognition
1718 Connecticut Avenue NW, Suite 500
Washington, DC 20009-1148
202-265-9090 800-424-4310

Family Resource Coalition (FRC)
200 South Michigan Avenue, Suite 1520
Chicago, IL 60604
312-341-0900

National Association for the Education of Young Children
(NAEYC)
1834 Connecticut Avenue NW
Washington, DC 20009-2460
202-232-8777 800-424-2460

National Head Start Association
201 North Union Street, Suite 320
Alexandria, VA 22314
703-739-0875

Appendix C

How *TLC* Addresses CDA Competencies

Competency Goal	CDA Unit	Functional Area	*TLC* Chapter
To support social and emotional development and provide positive guidance	Unit 4: Positive ways to support children's social and emotional development	Self	2: Building Self-Esteem Through Encouragement and Listening Skills
		Social	1: Understanding Children's Development and Behavior
			3. Solving Problems with Young Children
			5: Nurturing Emotional and Social Development
		Guidance	4: Cooperation and Discipline
To establish positive and productive relationships with families	Unit 6: Keys to establish productive relationships with families.	Families	6: Working in Partnership with Parents

Note: TLC also supplements training in the functional areas of Learning Environment, Cognitive, and Communication.

Glossary

Assets—skills or abilities

Brainstorming—a problem-solving technique in which people suggest as many ideas as possible. Evaluation of suggestions is delayed until all ideas are given.

Cognitive—Relating to the process of perceiving, thinking, knowing, remembering, and using information appropriately

Control—the need to feel in charge and to get one's own way

Developmentally appropriate—suited to child's intellectual, psychological, emotional, social, and physical stage of development

Developmentally incapable—intellectually, psychologically, emotionally, socially, or physically not yet able to perform a task or deal with a problem

Discipline—the methods used to teach children cooperative and responsible behavior

Discouragement—the reduction of self-esteem, confidence, and courage

Double standards—judging two individuals or groups according to different sets of expectations

Emotional thinking—thinking consciously about one's feelings

Empathize—to sincerely understand and communicate the understanding of another's feelings

Encouragement—building self-esteem through acceptance and confidence, focusing on assets, efforts, improvements, and contributions

Engagement—the stage of development in which a baby gains the ability to focus his or her attention and to interact with caring adults

Environment—the combination of the people and objects a child interacts with

Exploring alternatives—a five-step process of helping children look at different ways to solve a problem

External motivator—reinforcement given to a child for pleasing someone else (parent, teacher, etc.)

I-message—a statement made by a teacher or parent which explains, without judging or blaming, how the adult is affected by a behavior

Internal motivator—encouragement given to a child that increases the child's self-esteem and self-motivation

Logical consequence—the result of going against the rules of social cooperation

Martyr, being a—constantly feeling overresponsible and overburdened by others

Motor skills—physical abilities requiring a certain amount of strength, coordination, or dexterity. Large motor skills involve larger muscle groups, small motor skills involve smaller muscle groups.

Natural consequence—the result of going against the laws of nature

Negativism—a stage of development between babyhood and early childhood during which a child may often refuse to do what he or she is asked to do

Ownership (of a problem)—having the responsibility to solve the problem

Perfectionism—believing one needs to be perfect to gain acceptance or be in control

Personality priority—a chosen style of interacting with others in order to feel accepted or important

Pleasing—believing the way to relate well with others is to please people at all costs

Preverbal—not yet able to communicate through words

Punishment—a method of discipline that negatively affects a child's self-esteem (e.g., threats, yelling, put-downs)

Reflective listening—listening to what a child says, then stating what you believe the child is feeling, *reflecting* the emotions and the content of the child's message

Reinforcement—*any* recognition given to a child for performing a certain behavior. This recognition can be physical or emotional, and can be given intentionally or unconsciously by a teacher.

Role model—someone who sets an example for others

Self-discipline—the ability to make appropriate choices and take responsibility for one's own behavior

Self-esteem—a positive view of oneself—a positive self-image

Self-image—the opinion one has of oneself

Separation anxiety—a child's fear of not being with the parent or guardian (a parent or guardian can also experience separation anxiety when leaving a child)

Social interest—a willingness to cooperate with others and a desire to contribute to the common good

Temperament—the unique set of personality qualities and characteristics an individual child is born with

Time-out—a discipline method of temporarily excusing a very disruptive child from interacting with others, giving the child time to calm down

Transition time—the period of time when children are moving from one activity or location to another

Unconditionally valuable—valued equally with all others simply by being human—not by age, ability, or any other criteria

Victim, being a—believing others are responsible for one's own situation

You-message—a way of expressing negative feelings by criticizing or blaming the child

Index